SQUARING THE BLOCKCHAIN CIRCLE

SQUARING THE BLOCKCHAIN CIRCLE

Kunal Nandwani
www.kunalnandwani.com

THE BR✺WSER
Publishers and Booksellers
www.thebrowser.org

First Published in India by **The Browser**
(an imprint of J.G.S. Enterprises Pvt. Ltd.)
SCO 14-15, Sector 8-C, Chandigarh 160 009
Email: service@thebrowser.org

Copyright © 2019 Kunal Nandwani

ISBN 9781729319895

All Rights Reserved

THE BR☻WSER
www.thebrowser.org

Contents

Introduction — 1

Part I
The Invincible Ledger — 9
Genesis — 23
Breath of the Gods — 32
Cryptic Cryptos — 41

Part II
Blockchain 101 — 53
De.cen.tra.lis.ed — 68
Trust from Trustless — 79
Cracking Fort Knox — 88
The Scalability Trilemma — 98

Part III
Maslow's Hammer — 107
A Coin for your Thoughts — 124
Machines in the Anthropocene — 142

Introduction

The Whys and Wherefores

First, there was the blockchain. Then there was the hype. Now there's the hype surrounding the hype as almost all books, articles and talks commence by ritually declaring that there's a lot of hype around the blockchain. Since everyone agrees there is one, ergo, there must be one.

Dante Disparte in "Why Blockchain Why Now" (*Forbes*, April 2018):

> We are at the very crest of the blockchain hype cycle where there is a lot of sizzle, little steak and the occasional setback or indictments. All of this denotes progress.

Having paid obeisance at the altar of this hype-fog, this book slices through it in some detail. Is the blockchain something revolutionary in scope? Absolutely. Will it all play out in line with the way the investment dollars and resources are flowing? Not at all. Through this book, I offer a critique of the blockchain ecosystem, which along with Artificial Intelligence (AI), the Internet of Things (IoT) and advances in Quantum Computing is one of the critical drivers ushering in Web 3.0 and other futuristic changes.

Squaring the blockchain circle requires deconstructing some of our existing social and philosophical constructs, such as how we trust each other and how we arrive at the truth and then record it. There are also our economic and commercial constructs — the way we set up contracts and agreements and how we resolve our disputes. For centuries, these assumptions have been the edifice of our commerce and have changed little, or not at all, over time. The move from paper-based systems to digital systems and then onto the cloud never challenged these assumptions, just enhanced our capacity to process ever-increasing amounts of data more efficiently. Until about 2008 when the Global Financial Crisis (GFC) struck us.

The GFC and its aftermath exposed systemic flaws that brought the world economic order to the brink of collapse. Nations went bankrupt, currencies gyrated into a free fall, the world's biggest insurers failed, investment banks collapsed, and the central banks of the world faced a situation rapidly spiralling out of their control. While it is beyond the scope of this book to analyse the GFC and all its subsequent fall-out and developments, if it all had to be summed up in one line, that would have to be — the collapse of trust.

When trust collapsed, market liquidity evaporated. Blue-chip securities were suddenly unsellable. Bid-ask spreads shot through the roof, and even then there was no guarantee that the markets would absorb supply. Deals collapsed even before the ink was dry on the papers. Financial business came to a standstill, and the Federal Reserve Bank became the lender of last resort holding up the scaffolding and injecting liquidity through extraordinary measures.

It was against this background that in October that year (2008), forged in the smithy of the GFC, a person (or a group) called Satoshi Nakamoto published the Bitcoin white paper. It described the concept of a crypto currency — bitcoin — riding on an underlying technology, the blockchain, which could provide an alternative way to build trust, record truth, secure transactions and create a decentralised network spanning the globe outside the purview of any authority.

The initial interest it invoked was limited to a geeky group on the internet called the *Cypherpunks*, and the world hardly reacted. However, over the next five years, critical interest crossed the tipping point, and by 2017 a frenzy was underway. A significant part of the reason for the frenzy was the launch of another blockchain in 2014-15 called Ethereum which also permitted the creation of many other types of crypto currencies or digital tokens in addition to its native token called ether. The innovative idea of Initial Coin Offerings or ICOs resulted in some twenty billion dollars' worth of funds flowing into blockchain projects in a short time even as bubble indicators began flashing red all over. The success of bitcoin made blockchain into a household word and unleashed the power of human imagination regarding its applications. Bitcoin acquired the Midas touch.

If you pick any ten books on the subject of blockchains at random, you will come across an identical set of buzzwords describing the heart of this new technology: immutable, canonical, secure, decentralised, peer-to-peer, anonymous, trusted, transparent, distributed ledger or register. Indeed, the six blind men of Indostan would be pleasantly surprised at their unanimity in describing this beast (with apologies to John Godfrey Saxe).

But in the blockchain applications space, for all its frenzy and billions of committed project dollars, there is manifest blindness. Every industrial database seems to be a fit target for replacement by the blockchain, in a one-size-fits-all approach. A cost-benefit analysis is rarely demanded, and expectations ride sky-high. While I shall have no hesitation in decimating some of the half-baked and misconceived blockchain applications that are currently attracting large funding and attention, I believe in its power. Just not in the same way that is being touted.

Both governments and corporations, where centralisation is the mantra and anonymity anathema, have jumped onto the blockchain bandwagon as the next big thing. The stark contradictions in the strengths of the technology and its areas of application are entirely overlooked.

The real success stories of the blockchain as an applied technology so far are the crypto currencies bitcoin and ether, and the world is still coming to terms with their existence and volatile nature. All this even as smart operators have launched thousands of me-too digital tokens through ICOs in a bid to make hay while the bitcoin sun shines.

As technology companies, uTrade and Hashcove have been at the forefront of developing solutions based on blockchain for worldwide clients including consulting for governments. As the co-founder and CEO of uTrade and Hashcove, I have been a part of the euphoria surrounding this technology, as well as a student of its superb prowess. While I entertain no doubts about the success, longevity and transformative ability of the blockchain as a technology, I see it happening on a different trajectory from the one we are now on.

This book highlights that only a small percentage of the projects in the pipeline today are likely to deliver lasting value to their owners because of flawed assumptions. We are headed for a crash before things can normalise. Another premise is that those applications where the blockchain is a perfect fit will over time disrupt and disproportionately impact the rest of the ecosystem as the ripples (pun intended) spread far and wide, especially on the financial front.

I have divided this book into three parts.

The first part is the story of the origin of the blockchain and its enormous success culminating in the ICO boom. Recounted in four chapters, "The Invincible Ledger" expounds the age-old history and applications of ledgers in commerce and accounting and what makes the blockchain ledger so different, and well, invincible. It also describes how a ledger gave birth to a currency — an astonishing "Genesis" if there ever was one, which becomes the title of our second chapter, chronicling all the developments from the birth of the blockchain and bitcoins in their very first avatar by their inventor Satoshi Nakamoto. The second avatar of the blockchain came in the form of Ethereum and its token ether, and the chapter "Breath of the Gods" discusses changes in the underlying technology that made that such a huge success and brought into existence a new kind of application — the dApp. Finally, "Cryptic Cryptos", sub-titled "March of the Altcoins", takes an overview of how the bitcoin seed blossomed into a thousand different coins — crypto currencies with forks and transitions and variations around a theme.

The second part of the book discusses threadbare four specific and crucial aspects of blockchains — decentralisation, trust and truth, security and scalability — and zeroes in on what is feasible and probable as opposed to what is hyped and hoped. So "De.cen.tra.lis.ed" brings to the fore the paradox that to build a decentralised network, you cannot fully escape centralised governance. "Trust from Trustless" highlights the fact that while consensus protocols lay the foundation of trust, yet immutability cannot guarantee the truth and trust cannot bypass the "Oracle". Since a large part of this trust in blockchains emanates from their much-touted security strengths, "Cracking Fort Knox" debates their vulnerabilities in some detail. But of course, all trust and security is of limited use if the solution cannot be scaled to handle the task at hand, and "The Scalability Trilemma" devotes itself to this most crucial of aspects that the blockchain can only deliver on two out of its three key metrics (decentralisation, speed and security) at any given time. Readers not too well-versed with the technical terminology employed should take advantage of the introductory chapter in part II titled "Blockchain 101".

The last set of chapters in part three begins with "Maslow's Hammer" where the fallacy of viewing every database application as a nail for the blockchain hammer is exposed, the inevitable downside of any new technological breakthrough. For the average Joe and Jane, all the action lies in just the ICOs, which are the subject of "A Coin for your Thoughts". It debates the value embedded in crypto tokens, their mis-pricing and susceptibility to fraud, some of the emerging regulatory and management challenges, and the mainstreaming of blockchain applications. "Machines in the Anthropocene" views blockchain as a futuristic technology, the harbinger of "Web 3.0" and a pillar of some exciting transformations to come.

It is a truism that hindsight is 20/20, and it is only looking back from the vantage point of maybe a decade ahead would the actual impact of the blockchain be understood. Yet how can we resist the thrill and excitement of a revolution unfolding at lightspeed before our very eyes? If this book succeeds in engrossing you in the unfolding vision of things to come, but with your feet planted firmly on the ground, the blockchain circle will stand squared.

Kunal Nandwani
India, UK

As a matter of convention, throughout this book, Bitcoin (with a capital B) represents the underlying blockchain while bitcoin (with a small b) represents the digital token or crypto currency. Similar is the case with Ethereum, the blockchain and ether, the token.

Part I

The Invincible Ledger

How a Ledger Gave Birth to a Currency

Our ancestors said, "This is as good as written in stone." Our grandchildren will say, "It is as good as written on the blockchain."
— Andreas M. Antonopoulos, *The Internet of Money*

A ledger is a ledger is a ledger. At heart, it is merely a record of a series of relevant transactions in time. You can maintain one on a piece of paper or tap it into a computer database or write it to the blockchain. Why then is the blockchain ledger — in essence a "distributed" database — such a big deal?

Ledgers have been used to keep accounts and records for thousands of years. The ancient Babylonians figured out how to record who owed whom how much and wrote them on elaborate clay-tablets using columns and symbols when paper did not even exist. Italian merchants used Venetian ledgers based on a then-revolutionary double-entry accounting system codified by Luca Pacioli in 1494, and it is something we still use today to make modern commerce possible.

To elaborate a little, a firm selling goods to a regular business client would like to keep a record of all products invoiced in the client's "ledger" by date. It would also record therein all payments received from the client, and adjustments on account of rejections, discounts or overheads. Hence, at any point in time, the firm would know what the client owes it. The client would maintain a similar ledger at their end, and there may be a periodic reconciliation process put in place to ensure that the client's and the firm's ledger match to avoid any disputes. It may also be the case that one or both sets of ledgers are subject to periodic audit by outside agencies to ensure the integrity of the accounting process.

Another example of a ledger's use would be the title records of a property that changes hands over time. Since there are taxes to be paid each time a property is bought, sold or inherited, the government has a vested interest in maintaining an accurate ledger of all such transactions.

Banks must capture transactions of their depositors and borrowers, hospitals must maintain patient history, a lawyer needs her case records to succeed, and the police would like to keep track of a criminal's record over time. All these are but applications of ledgers. In an over-simplified way, a ledger may be equated with an excel sheet or a database table with records representing each transaction in order of date and time.

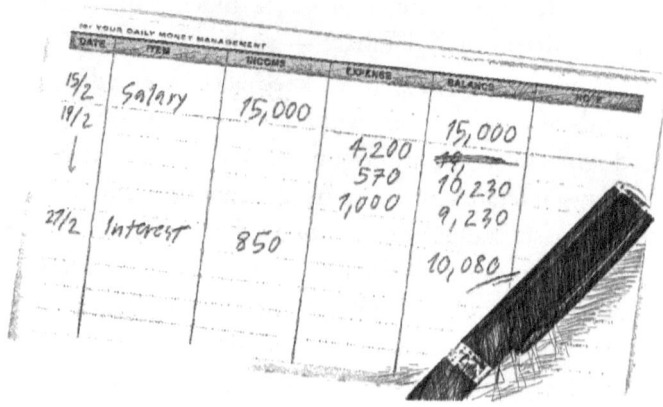

Simple Home Ledger — Date-wise Income and Expenses

Three questions then spring to the mind — who updates and maintains the ledgers, how to trust the accuracy of their contents, and what if someone tampers with them? The answer to these three questions separates a blockchain ledger from the rest and makes it a really, really big deal.

Traditional Ledger Design

To understand traditional ledger design better, let us take it for granted that the ledger recording a set of transactions is maintained digitally on a network of computers in database tables.

We begin by differentiating between the front-end controlling authority which owns and operates the ledger, let's call it the "Master"; and the backend software-hardware architecture of the database system which records the data of the ledger, let's call it the "Recorder" (how brilliant is that!).

In such a setup, both the Master and the Recorder are centralised entities. The Master could be a government agency, a body or association, a corporation or an individual, and it may be considered decentralised in a minimal sense if the rights to operate the ledger, initiate and authorise transactions are delegated to a group of employees or some third-parties on behalf of the owner. The ledger's viewing rights could also be private or public as required. But the critical inference here is that members of the public at large cannot initiate or update a ledger transaction on their own.

As far the Recorder goes, the traditional setup is that of a client-server architecture on a network of computers (maybe the internet) with multiple clients (or browsers) sending in requests to a central database server which then executes the requests and sends back data or confirmation. The client-server database architecture has long served as a strong backbone of the web with significant strides in performance and optimisation over time. A typical ERP application is an excellent example of such an architecture where various front-end client machines send in the requests to the backend database.

Client-Server Configuration
The Master authorises several Clients to update transactions on its behalf on the central Server (Recorder)

So a typical transaction would consist of the Master initiating one over the network, authorising it and sending the authenticated data to the Recorder for capture and confirmation of the same. The Master would also have the authority to edit or delete existing data in the Recorder.

As would be evident to an astute reader, the pitfalls of centralisation would apply to both the front-end Master and backend Recorder. Take security, for instance. If the Master is compromised, an unauthorised agent could gain rights to play havoc with the recorded transactions. Or an agent may directly hack into the Recorder and gain control of the database. Either way, even if there is a single point of failure, the entire ledger stands compromised.

Now, if either the Master, or the Recorder, or both, were to be "decentralised", the end result would be a more secure, fault-tolerant and robust system (the subtler meaning of what decentralisation implies is examined in its namesake chapter, but for now it is interpreted in the usual English sense as something not centralised). For example, large parts of the Amazon AWS network are decentralised both architecturally and geographically, so a Recorder (database) hosted on the AWS network will automatically derive these benefits, and the failure of any one computer, or even multiple computers, will not halt any operations.

However, decentralising the Master is easier said than done as the final control of the database must rest somewhere. Multiple masters, who can individually overwrite each other's records at will, can endanger the integrity of the ledger if not handled with caution and adequate safeguards at the design stage itself.

Blockchain Ledger Design

A blockchain is primarily formed and driven by a piece of open-source software — an algorithm — that any participating computer (called a node) on the internet can download and run. Each new node that plugs into the network and runs this program is furnished a copy of an entire existing "ledger" immediately, in a pre-decided format and way as per the blockchain's algorithm's "protocol", to be downloaded and then kept updated.

All nodes are peers.

The protocol is a set of special rules that nodes in a blockchain network use when they transmit or receive information. Besides, it controls all other aspects of the blockchain that are explained in the succeeding paragraphs such as the operation of special nodes called "miners" and consensus formation by them across the network. The protocol lies at the heart of the blockchain design and it determines the strengths and weaknesses of the latter.

14 | Squaring the Blockchain Circle

A Peer-to-Peer Network
Each node in the blockchain is both a Client, a Server and some special nodes may opt to become Miners

So what are the "transactions" contained in this downloaded blockchain "ledger", and how is a new transaction recorded on it?

To answer that, we must look at another component — "digital tokens" — created by the blockchain algorithm itself, again as per the protocol forming part of the program design. The ledger of the blockchain is a record of transferring these digital tokens from one "account" to another "account" with the passage of time.

And the next obvious question will be — how did it all start?

It stands to reason that a certain number of digital tokens come into existence ab initio when the blockchain is created by the first node for transactions to start, and more tokens are generated later, depending on the protocol and algorithm design. The ab initio tokens created are then allocated to one or more pre-existing "accounts" (again ab initio) which is what the ledger would record in the first instance.

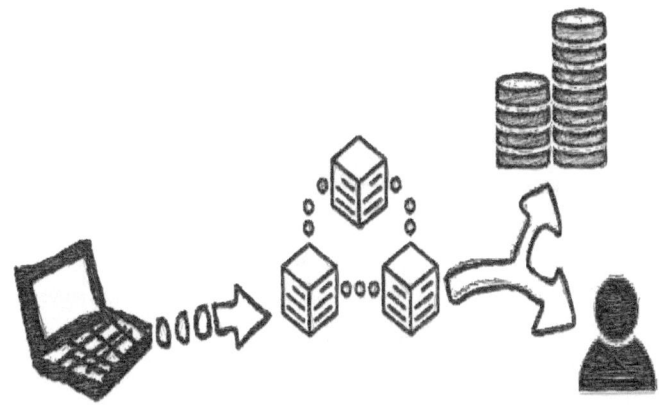

The Blockchain Protocol
It creates the first (pre)mined pool of digital tokens and the first user account(s) to hold these tokens to begin transactions

As tokens are transferred from one account to the other by their respective account-holders, these make up the initial "transactions" on the blockchain and are recorded in the ledger. New tokens that come into existence, later on, are also allocated to some accounts, and the same are also recorded in the ledger. Since anyone is free to create an account on the blockchain and receive tokens from an existing account holder, and having received them, send them to still others, the chain of transfers continues. An account is created using a "client" software on the node and accounts can be mapped to a "digital wallet" software to hold the tokens.

The beauty of this token system is that any arbitrary data can be appended and stored with the digital tokens themselves; hence the tokens can be equated with anything, like property titles, for instance. Thus a transfer of a token from one account to another may represent the transfer of the corresponding property title from one account holder to the other in the real world.

Besides storing a copy of the ledger, each node in the network can function both as a client and a server. It can create new requests for adding records, and process requests initiated by other nodes. No Master controls these nodes.

New additions to records in the ledger are based on a somewhat elaborate "consensus" algorithm running on certain nodes called "miners", who opt to run it, and then broadcast the result to the remaining nodes for updating their copies. A new record may be added to the ledger if over 51% of the nodes agree, and it gets appended at the end of the existing chain of records. Once appended, no record may ever be deleted or modified.

Tying all this together to make it possible, the blockchain algorithm incentivises and recognises the additional computational work performed by the "miners". It does this by creating new digital tokens on the network and doles them out as per protocol as rewards to the miners. Any node can choose to be a miner for as long as it likes and competes against other miners to gather these reward tokens by authenticating transactions.

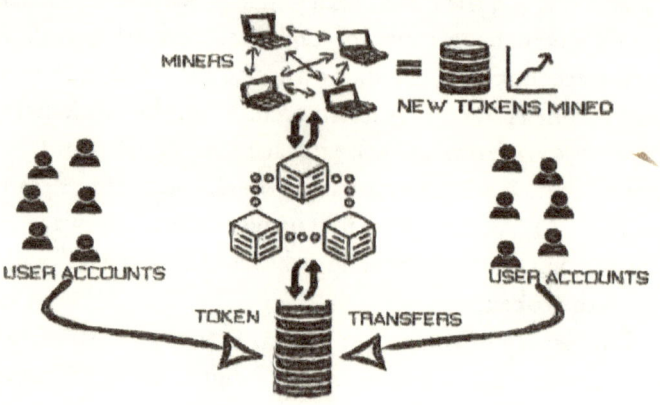

Transactions on a Blockchain
User Requests to transfer tokens between accounts are validated by the Miners who in turn earn reward tokens as per the blockchain protocol

The blockchain thus makes it possible to dispense with the ideas of a Master and Recorder altogether while creating and maintaining a ledger. Architecturally, the network of participating nodes is not just a decentralised entity, but a distributed one too, since each node could be located anywhere on the internet, and it stores a full copy of the ledger as a peer of every other node, resulting in distributed storage of data.

To put it in layman terms, at the risk of repetition, a blockchain is a special ledger "out there on the internet" which no one owns or controls and which anyone can download (using opensource client software). A free account can be created on it to receive/send digital blockchain tokens from/to other accounts, and such transactions can be appended to the blockchain ledger after validation by majority of the participating computers in the network. Once added, transactions cannot be deleted or amended. Designated computers (the miners) facilitate the validation process and get newly-minted digital tokens as rewards which are created by the blockchain software. More the tokens that move between accounts, more are the transactions that need validation, and more new tokens get minted and rewarded to the miners, increasing the total digital tokens in circulation in a self-reinforcing loop.

Blockchain to Crypto currency to Crypto economics

Now here's the real twist to the tale. If there is a cap within the blockchain design on the total number of digital tokens that can be mined, and if all account-holders treat these tokens as a (crypto) currency, voila, the ledger itself is acting like a bank, recording currency transfers between accounts which then become immutable. If you set up exchanges to convert the crypto currency with real-world currencies like the USD, and the market arrives at a consensus exchange rate, you have created a bridge to real-economy transactions as well.

The logical question is why people would treat digital tokens generated by a software program as a currency? And the most straightforward answer is: why not?

Because at heart, and the world over, an everyday fiat currency like the USD is nothing but a piece of paper (a paper token) issued by a central bank like the Federal Reserve which declares it to have a value (say a hundred dollars) to which people agree and repose their trust in. And although the digital token is a software creation and not issued by a bank, as long as people agree and repose confidence in the token's value and the soundness of the technology of the blockchain platform (which replaces the central bank), the digital token works successfully as a currency. Since it is a digital product, it brings certain additional qualities which even fiat currencies cannot match, such as instant borderless transfers across the world, anonymous accounts, negligible transfer costs, etcetera.

Even if you compare digital tokens with a commodity like gold, which has been extensively used as a currency in history, the parallels still hold good. Just as gold is scarce and mined, the number of tokens is also capped and require mining. Just as the market accords an exchange value to gold vis-à-vis other commodities and currencies, so does the market accord value to these tokens. And just as gold has certain advantages over other commodities while serving as a currency, such as that it is divisible, transferable, keeps its purity, etcetera so also the tokens have many advantages already enumerated.

History is littered with commodities that have been currencies in various societies at various times, including one remarkable example in the following section. From the perspective of the traditional theory of currency — which states a currency should act as a means of exchange, a storehouse of value and a unit of account — many currencies have had unique characteristics which these three roles never quite captured. Digital tokens as currencies are at the start of their evolutionary journey, and they possess features that no traditional commodity or fiat currency has ever had. Hence, they will chart their course of economic evolution transforming commerce, society and politics in their image — giving rise to the emerging field of "crypto economics".

Even more significantly, anyone can build and launch many such blockchains "out there on the internet". Some will achieve a critical mass in terms of users and accounts while others will fail. They may use different underlying technologies in how to post and validate transactions, how to generate their digital tokens or "mine" them, and differ in their strengths and weaknesses and additional features. Adam Smith's "invisible hand" is free to decide the outcome.

Just as you can build new program layers on top of an existing software layer, the blockchain, being a software, is no exception. So not only can you launch a new token (or crypto currency) on top of a current token, you can also build other programs triggered to execute automatically when a new transaction occurs on the blockchain.

Historically, it is pertinent to note that the blockchain does not represent the first attempt at building a digital currency or electronic cash. The problem facing all previous efforts which the blockchain design solved for the first time is known as the "double spend" problem. Since a digital currency is just a digital file, nothing prevents anybody from copying it many times over and sharing it with different people, which in money talk would amount to counterfeiting digital money or spending the same digital coin multiple times. The blockchain solved this problem by creating a mechanism to verify each transaction through its mining and consensus algorithms without the need for a central trusted authority like a central bank, thus preventing counterfeit transactions from being authenticated and recorded. The blockchain polices itself to catch thieves and fraudsters on its network.

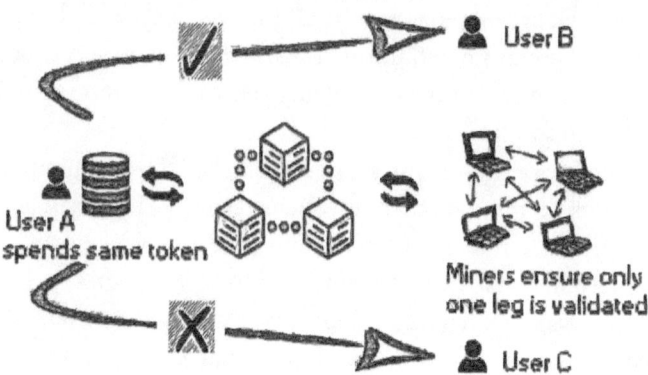

Double Spend Problem
Miners ensure that no digital token is double spent while validating the transaction on the Blockchain

A Blockchain in History

Although blockchains represent cutting-edge digital technology, a dip into history is not only a revelation but a succinct explanation of how blockchains work. People of the Yap Island in the Micronesian islands used stones called Rai or Fei as currency — not common stones but large circular stone-discs carved from limestone with a hole in the middle, like massive doughnuts, weighing up to 4000 kg. Owing to the bulk and unwieldy nature of these stones, the Yapeses could not move these easily, and transactions between their people were conducted based on an oral history of ownership of the stones. Items were bought and sold by agreeing that the ownership of a particular stone had changed. They then made this knowledge familiar within the tribe by oral transmission, and every tribe member virtually knew the ownership of every stone. The practice, which may well be over a thousand years old, was still in use when the twentieth century began. The parallels to the blockchain are undeniable and exciting — the mental record of the ownership history of all stones amounts to a distributed ledger held by each tribal acting as a node in the network. Whenever a transaction occurs, there is a "broadcast", and if there is a dispute, the majority opinion about the ownership prevails (a consensus mechanism) to arrive at the truth. Ancient becomes the new modern in bits and bytes.

The Sum of its Parts

Since the whole is always more than the sum of its parts, the beauty of the blockchain is that it creates a powerful new ecosystem to make applications that could not have existed before. Vitalik Buterin, the blockchain pioneer, evangelist and co-founder of Ethereum, saw this possibility and enabled the design of autonomous programs that could execute on the blockchain nodes when triggered, which he termed as *Smart Contracts*. When asked for a best short explanation of the blockchain (Conversations with Tyler — Vitalik Buterin as transcribed on Medium.com, July 2018), he stated:

> One of the analogies I keep going back to is this idea of a "world computer." The idea, basically, is that a blockchain, as a whole, functions like a computer. It has a hard drive, and on that hard drive, it stores what all the accounts are.
>
> It stores what the code of all the smart contracts is, what the memory of all these smart contracts is. It accepts incoming instructions—and these incoming instructions are signed transactions sent by a bunch of different users—and processes them according to a set of rules.
>
> On a blockchain, you can ultimately build anything that you can build on top of a computer. From a computer science theoretical point of view, in terms of what it provides, you can think about it as being a computer.

But what it provides on top of that is these extra trust guarantees: the guarantee that the computer will run in the way that you expect it to run, and that a few people can't make that guarantee fail by going out of business, getting hacked, dying, having their company go bankrupt, deciding to be evil one day, deciding they have some monopolistic interest to start acting differently one day, and all of those different issues.

The promise of an invincible ledger, layered with executable programs, which overcomes the drawbacks of existing systems and architectures is the basis of the blockchain euphoria, and why there is this mad race to migrate existing applications to the blockchain, without stopping to examine the merits or demerits of such a move. It's the reason people poured their savings into crypto currencies — money they could never see — because they believed the blockchain would never fail them. It's why there is the buzz of smart contracts, autonomous applications, machine-to-machine micropayments and a transformation in the engines of commerce.

But is this ledger really invincible? Are the contracts truly smart? That is the answer we derive as we square each aspect of the blockchain circle — decentralisation, trust and truth, security and scalability — one at a time.

But we're getting ahead of our story, which begins with the Bitcoin and its shadowy inventor Satoshi Nakamoto.

Genesis

The Birth of Bitcoin

> It's either going to change everything, or nothing.
> — Nathaniel Popper, *Digital Gold: Bitcoin and the Inside Story of the Misfits and Millionaires Trying to Reinvent Money*

When Satoshi Nakamoto's fingers deftly tapped on a keyboard on Jan 3, 2009, mining the "genesis block" (number 0) to launch the first blockchain known to humankind called Bitcoin, he gave himself a reward of 50 digital tokens he called, well, bitcoins. Then on Jan 12, he sent a gift of 10 bitcoins to Hal Finney, recording the first bitcoin transaction on the newly born Bitcoin blockchain.

The Cypherpunks

Along with Finney, two early supporters of bitcoin were Wei Dai and Nick Szabo, all pioneers working towards the development of crypto currencies. As early as 1997, a Dr Adam Back had created an anonymous transacting system called Hashcash, similar to a 1992 Proof-of-Work consensus protocol developed by Dwork and Naor. In the following year, Wei Dai published a proposal for B-money, and one of his methods of maintaining transaction data became known as Proof-of-Stake, later adopted by the Ethereum blockchain. Hal Finney, in 2004, created Reusable Proofs-of-Work based on some ideas from HashCash, and Nick Szabo in 2005 further built upon Finney's and other approaches to come up with a crypto currency called Bitgold.

Finney, Dai and Szabo were all members of a group which identified themselves as *Cypherpunks* — activists advocating the widespread use of strong cryptography and privacy enhancing technologies as a route to social and political change (Wikipedia). *The Cypherpunk Manifesto* written by Eric Hughes in 1993 defines the fundamental principles underlying this movement.

It was to the *Cypherpunk* mailing list that the pseudonymous Nakamoto sent a paper — "Bitcoin: A Peer-to-Peer Electronic Cash System" — which referred to B-money and Hashcash.

Finney, in his forum post "Bitcoin and Me" (Mar 19, 2013*)*, sums up the early journey of bitcoin from his perspective:

> I thought I'd write about the last four years, an eventful time for Bitcoin and me.
> For those who don't know me, I'm Hal Finney. I got my start in crypto working on an early version of PGP, working closely with Phil Zimmermann. When Phil decided to start PGP Corporation, I was one of the first hires. I would work on PGP until my retirement. At the same time, I got involved with the Cypherpunks. I ran the first cryptographically based anonymous re-mailer, among other activities.
> Fast forward to late 2008 and the announcement of Bitcoin. I've noticed that cryptographic greybeards (I was in my mid-50's) tend to get cynical. I was more idealistic; I have always loved crypto, the mystery and the paradox of it.
> When Satoshi announced Bitcoin on the cryptography

mailing list, he got a sceptical reception at best. Cryptographers have seen too many grand schemes by clueless noobs. They tend to have a knee-jerk reaction.

I was more positive. I had long been interested in cryptographic payment schemes. Plus I was lucky enough to meet and extensively correspond with both Wei Dai and Nick Szabo, generally acknowledged to have created ideas that would be realised with Bitcoin. I had made an attempt to create my own proof-of-work based currency, called RPOW. So I found Bitcoin fascinating.

When Satoshi announced the first release of the software, I grabbed it right away. I think I was the first person besides Satoshi to run bitcoin. I mined block 70-something, and I was the recipient of the first bitcoin transaction, when Satoshi sent ten coins to me as a test. I carried on an email conversation with Satoshi over the next few days, mostly me reporting bugs and him fixing them.

Today, Satoshi's true identity has become a mystery. But at the time, I thought I was dealing with a young man of Japanese ancestry who was very smart and sincere. I've had the good fortune to know many brilliant people over the course of my life, so I recognise the signs.

After a few days, bitcoin was running pretty stable, so I left it running. Those were the days when difficulty was 1, and you could find blocks with a CPU, not even a GPU. I mined several blocks over the next days. But I turned it off because it made my computer run hot, and the fan noise bothered me. In retrospect, I wish I had kept it up longer, but on the other hand I was extraordinarily lucky to be there at the beginning. It's one of those glass half full half empty things.

The next I heard of Bitcoin was late 2010, when I was surprised to find that it was not only still going, bitcoins actually had a monetary value. I dusted off my old wallet and was relieved to discover that my bitcoins were still there. As the price climbed up to real money, I transferred the coins into an offline wallet where hopefully they'll be worth something to my heirs.

Finney passed away in Phoenix in Aug 2014, having been diagnosed in 2009 with ALS, a fatal motor neuron disease.

The Rise 2009-16

In the early days, it is estimated that Nakamoto mined one million bitcoins, before disappearing and handing over the reins to developer Gavin Andresen who then became the bitcoin lead developer at the Bitcoin Foundation.

At that time, it was still possible to mine bitcoins using the CPU of any basic computer, and between 2009-10 many early bitcoin adopters could amass a lot of bitcoins this way. Then GPUs (Graphic Processing Units) became the new standard for mining and thus the bitcoin mining race began accelerating. Around 2011, some miners switched from GPUs to FPGAs (Field Programmable Gate Arrays), after the first implementation of Bitcoin mining came out in Verilog (a hardware design language that's used to program FPGAs). FPGA mining was a rather short-lived phenomenon, and while GPU mining dominated for about a year, the days of FPGA mining were far more limited — lasting only a few months before custom ASICs (Application Specific Integrated Circuits) arrived.

Bitcoin mining is now heavily centralised and monopolised by large mining facilities around the world, especially in China. Each new block earns its miner a reward, which started at 50 bitcoins in 2009 and was programmed to halve every four years, and is currently at 12.5 bitcoins, or around US$ 80,000. These block rewards are the only source of new bitcoins in the system.

The first bitcoin transactions were between individuals on the bitcoin forum, and someone paid 10,000 BTC to purchase indirectly two pizzas delivered by Papa John's Pizza.

It was a matter of time before the idea to establish a market platform for trading bitcoins like any other currency would arise, giving rise to the bitcoin exchanges — the first crypto currency exchange platforms. One of the earliest of such platforms was Mt. Gox established in 2010. A major contributing factor to popularity of bitcoin around this time were activities of the "dark web" — services like Silk Road, AlphaBay and Hansa — all of which were marketplaces for illicit items. Bitcoin was a popular currency on these platforms due to its anonymous nature.

In the spring of 2011, the market price of bitcoin was pegged at around $2 when some people began investing heavily in it. WikiLeaks and other organisations accepted bitcoins for donations in June that year, while in September, Vitalik Buterin co-founded the *Bitcoin Magazine*. Things picked up momentum in 2012 as BitPay reported having over 1,000 merchants accepting bitcoin under its payment processing service, and WordPress too accepted bitcoins.

February 2013 saw bitcoin-based payment processor Coinbase report a sale of over US$1 million worth of bitcoins in a single month at over US $22 per bitcoin. The Winklevoss twins Cameron and Tyler, who had sued Mark Zuckerberg and Facebook, bought US $11 million worth of bitcoin. By then the price of bitcoin was US $110. More people were putting six-figure and seven-figure sums into the bitcoin market and driving up the prices.

Two companies, Robocoin and Bitcoiniacs, launched the world's first bitcoin ATM on October 29, 2013, in Vancouver, BC, Canada, allowing clients to sell or purchase bitcoin currency at a downtown coffee shop. Chinese internet giant Baidu allowed clients to pay with bitcoins. The Internet Archive announced that it was ready to accept donations as bitcoins and that it intended to give employees the option to receive portions of their salaries in bitcoins as well. In November, the University of Nicosia announced that it would accept bitcoin as payment for tuition fees, with the university's chief financial officer calling it the "gold of tomorrow".

Around that time, the China-based bitcoin exchange BTC China overtook the Japan-based Mt. Gox and the Europe-based Bitstamp to become the largest bitcoin trading exchange by trade volume. But on December 5, the People's Bank of China prohibited Chinese financial institutions from using bitcoins, and Baidu no longer accepted bitcoins for its services. Overall, from mid-2013 to mid-2014, China went from a negligible share of bitcoin trading to virtually the entire market.

Bitcoin's early history coincided and got forever embroiled with that of the Silk Road — an online black market founded in early 2011 and a part of what became known as the "dark web" — dealing in illegal drugs, contraband and merchandise. Bitcoin became the sole mode of purchase on the Silk Road which hit an annual turnover exceeding $15 million, and when the FBI cracked down on it in late 2013, it made huge seizures of bitcoins from Silk Road's accounts. It cemented the "bitcoin is for criminals" image in the minds of many. Even after the dismantling of Silk Road, many dark market copycats sprang up using bitcoins as their mode of payment.

When in Sep 2014, TeraExchange LLC, received an approval from the U.S. Commodity Futures Trading Commission (CFTC) to list an over-the-counter swap product based on the price of a bitcoin, it marked the first time a U.S. regulatory agency approved a bitcoin financial product. Microsoft began accepting bitcoins in December that year to let people buy its Xbox games and Windows software, and in January 2015, Coinbase raised US$75 million as part of a Series C funding, the highest ever for a bitcoin company. Barclays announced that they would become the first UK high street bank to accept bitcoins.

The period from 2014 to 16 remained one of Chinese hegemony over the bitcoin space in-spite of their government's clampdown banning their banks from engaging in bitcoin transactions. This could be attributed to Chinese dominance of bitcoin mining wherein miners would have to sell their newly minted bitcoins.

By spring 2016, a massive chunk of the bitcoin market shifted to Japan when its government recognised virtual currencies like bitcoin officially in March that year. The Japanese Yen became bitcoin's biggest trading partner, a lead it still maintains. Uber announced the use of bitcoin in Argentina. By September, there were over 771 bitcoin ATMs worldwide. Swiss Railways (SBB) upgraded their ATMs to be bitcoin compatible.

The Breaches

Security challenges emerged as the first significant breach in bitcoin's history occurred on Aug 15, 2010, when over 184 billion bitcoins generated in a transaction were sent to two addresses. There was a flaw that allowed this to happen which had been discovered on Aug 6 itself, but a delay in fixing the bug caused the breach. It was corrected in the only possible manner by "forking" the network and updating the version of the bitcoin protocol (forking is explained in some detail in the chapter *Blockchain 101* in Part II of this book).

Another problem arose on Mar 12, 2013, when a bitcoin miner running version 0.8.0 of the bitcoin software created a large block considered invalid in version 0.7 (due to an undiscovered inconsistency between the two versions), creating another "fork" in the blockchain. As a result, two separate transaction logs formed without a clear consensus, but miners resolved this by downgrading to version 0.7, putting them back on track with the canonical blockchain, and the network reached a consensus and continued to operate as usual a few hours after the split.

Then in 2014, one of the most devastating hacks in the crypto currency market occurred on the Mt. Gox platform resulting in the theft of 744,408 BTC, and along with the collapse of the Silk Road dark marketplace around the same time, it almost brought the entire bitcoin market to its knees.

Less than a year later, the United Kingdom-based exchange Bitstamp went offline for several days while they investigated a hack in which about 19,000 bitcoins were stolen from their wallet.

In August 2016, a major bitcoin exchange, Bitfinex, was hacked and nearly 120,000 BTC were stolen.

The Boom 2017-18

On August 1, 2017 bitcoin hard-forked into two derivative digital currencies, the bitcoin (BTC) blockchain with a 1 MB blocksize limit and the Bitcoin Cash (BCH) blockchain with an 8 MB blocksize limit.

Around May 2017, the price of bitcoin (BTC) crossed US$2000 for the very first time, rising to US$3000 just weeks later. By September, it had scaled past US$5000 culminating in an all-time high price of US$19783.21 in December 2017, followed by a 30% drop within days. The volatility was, and is, palpable. For most of 2018, its value has ranged between US$6000 to about US$8000.

Analysts have attributed many overlapping causes for this boom — from outright speculative mania to a general mistrust in governments across the world, to anti-institutional investors, and to hedgers trying to protect themselves against a repeat of the Global Financial Crisis of 2008. The political environment of the US in particular, under President Trump, is also cited as a significant cause. There is also the thesis that the generational shift has played an enormous role with Millennials showing higher interest in bitcoins rather than in owning stocks.

While naysayers pronounce that the bitcoin bubble is ready to burst, there are as many who believe the boom has a long way to go and that this is just the beginning. There is even a particular term for bitcoin hoarding by believers and fanatics — HODL — or hold on for dear life.

In hindsight, no one could have imagined that people all over the world would give away real money for a digital currency whose network nobody owns, no central bank guarantees it, is not backed by gold or any other asset, is not even accepted for most real-world products and services, is actively discouraged by many governments and is lost forever if an account key is lost.

There is nothing comparable to the bitcoin in terms of a global currency, and if one considers similar efforts for a broad-based multi-nation currency such as the Euro, it is clear that such projects take decades of effort, negotiations and cajoling to be acceptable, and then forever remain at the risk of unravelling, as evidenced by the Greek crisis and then Brexit. In contrast, an unknown Satoshi Nakamoto brought together users from all over the world to repose trust in a non-state/non-gold-backed digital currency and the world's first digitally scarce asset within a few years of its inception.

Even as bitcoin flourished — it remains the star crypto currency even today — a 17-year-old caused a stir with his blockchain design and its token which he named the Breath of the Gods, or Ether. His design was preceded by the work of yet another man who virtually invented the concept of the Initial Coin Offering (ICO) — a precursor to the frenzy that was in the making. While the following chapter is their story, the ICO boom made bitcoin the default gateway currency to invest in these tokens thus cementing it as their leader.

Breath of the Gods

The Story of Ethereum

> Bitcoin is great as a form of digital money, but its scripting language is too weak for any kind of serious advanced applications to be built on top
> — Vitalik Buterin, co-founder of Ethereum

Nakamoto, in his blog-post announcing the launch of Bitcoin, had called it "a new open source P2P e-cash system". His vision, like that of the *Cypherpunks*, was that of a crypto currency transcending the limits of any fiat currency. But his invention — the Bitcoin blockchain incentivised by the bitcoin tokens — set other people thinking. What if the blockchain technology was de-coupled from its crypto currency use-case? Could it have other applications as well? And the result of these thoughts was something outstanding — leading to the birth of the blockchain Ethereum and its concept of *Smart Contracts* (autonomous programs hosted and executed on the blockchain itself) and culminating in the tremendous crypto-ICO boom.

ICO #1

This part of the story begins at a Bitcoin conference in San

Jose in 2013, where a panellist J.R. Willet, first spoke about his ideas:

> If you wanted to, today, start a new protocol layer on top of Bitcoin, a lot of people don't realise, you could do it without going to a bunch of venture capitalists and instead of saying, hey, I've got this idea, you can — you're familiar with Kickstarter I assume? Most of you? You can actually say, okay, here's my pitch, here's my group of developers — there's a lot of developers in this room. If you get a bunch of trustworthy guys together that people have heard of and say, okay, we're going to do this. We're going to make a new protocol layer. It's going to have new features X, Y and Z on top of bitcoin, and here's who we are and here's our plan, and here's our bitcoin address, and anybody who sends coins to this address owns a piece of our new protocol. Anybody could do that. And I've been telling people this for at least a year now because I want to invest in it. I don't have a ton of coins, but that's where I want to invest my coins. And I've yet to find somebody who wants my coins.

Willett had already published a white paper about this in Jan 2012 which he titled *The Second Bitcoin White Paper*, and where he stated that "We claim that the existing Bitcoin network can be used as a protocol layer, on top of which new currency layers with new rules can be built without changing the foundation".

His idea gave birth to what we call as the ICO — Initial Coin Offering — which is primarily an advance sale of a project's crypto currency or token, to be used within the platform or outside to fund the development of the platform. Willett also launched the first-ever ICO in 2013 and called it Mastercoin, raising $500,000 worth of bitcoins.

Vitalik Buterin, a 17-year-old programmer at that time, was genuinely intrigued by blockchain technology when he got involved in Bitcoin and became a contributor to its code base.

He also co-founded the *Bitcoin Magazine* in 2011. Writing an op-ed piece in his magazine titled *Mastercoin: A Second-Generation Protocol on the Bitcoin Blockchain* (Nov 4, 2013), Buterin sheds light on his appreciation of Willett's ideas:

> The concept of an alternative currently relying on Bitcoin to take advantage of its powerful and secure network backed by petahashes of mining power is not a new idea. The general concept first appeared in a much weaker form as "merged mining", a mechanism in which alternative currency miners publish pointers to their blocks in the Bitcoin blockchain to mitigate the threat of 51% attacks. Mastercoin, however, takes this principle a step further. Rather than simply using the Bitcoin blockchain as a secure timestamping system to store its own blocks, Mastercoin uses the Bitcoin blockchain to store every transaction. Philosophically, the best way to think of Mastercoin is as an alternative way of making sense of Bitcoin transactions; just like the Bitcoin protocol takes a series of transactions and parses them to determine how many bitcoins are in every address at any particular moment, the Mastercoin protocol also takes the available Bitcoin transactions and parses them to extract data relevant to the Mastercoin network.
>
> ...
>
> From a less philosophical standpoint, the practical advantages that a Mastercoin protocol has on top of Bitcoin are essentially twofold. First, Mastercoin can leverage the high degree of security that the Bitcoin network gains from its popularity and its high level of mining power. Second, it becomes much easier to create protocols that interact between Bitcoin and Mastercoin, and potentially with other on-blockchain protocols to come in the future.
>
> ...
>
> One problem that many have with Mastercoin as it stands is that, in some ways, Mastercoin is much more centralised than more standard crypto currencies such as Bitcoin, Litecoin and Primecoin. Unlike these more standard crypto

currencies, where everyone has a chance to earn coins by a neutral process of computational mining, in Mastercoin all mastercoins were initially issued to users who donated money to the Mastercoin Foundation's Exodus address.

...

Many Bitcoin users do not like pre-mines because there is a strong belief that the whole point of crypto currencies is that they are decentralised, and thus a true crypto currency should not privilege any specific centralised parties in any way. It is true that Mastercoin's issuance model is not like Ripple's, in the sense that there is no central party that started out owning any mastercoins by default. Furthermore, on a practical level, Ripple Labs is a private corporation, whereas the Mastercoin Foundation is a non-profit organisation and a silver-level business member of the Bitcoin Foundation. However, the Mastercoin Foundation is nevertheless a privileged party, as no one else had the ability to earn BTC from the issuing process. Furthermore, with the way the protocol is organised now, the Mastercoin Foundation is entitled to extract ~1.2 cents from the marker output in every transaction in perpetuity. Both the centralised issuance and the ongoing privileged status that the Mastercoin protocol gives to this one organisation, many Bitcoin users believe, disqualifies Mastercoin from being classified as a truly decentralised currency.

Buterin visualised an even more powerful platform that would go beyond the currency transfer use-case of Bitcoin and released a white paper in 2013 describing his ideas. It included the concept of immutable autonomous contracts executing on the blockchain which anyone could code.

The simple proposition was — instead of having lots of application-specific blockchains, why not have a single public blockchain that could be programmed to do whatever was necessary and remain infinitely extensible. He called his blockchain as Ethereum and its digital token as ether — what the ancient Greeks called the breath of the gods, believing its pure essence filled the space outside the mortal world, and embodying it as the fifth element that along with earth, water, air and fire made up the building blocks of all creation.

DApps on the Blockchain

Although bitcoin was and is a success, its two limitations were clear to Buterin — that it was slow, validating transactions roughly every ten minutes, and that its protocol was hard to update and improve since it depended on a small group of developers who could do so. He wanted to build a blockchain that could validate faster, and could store other information apart from that related to transfer of digital tokens, and could play host to small computer programs written to perform specific actions. These would take the shape of "smart contracts" or "decentralised applications" (dApps).

To quote from his *The Ethereum White Paper* (https://github.com/ethereum/wiki/wiki/White-Paper):

> The intent of Ethereum is to create an alternative protocol for building decentralised applications, providing a different set of trade-offs that we believe will be very useful for a large class of decentralised applications, with particular emphasis on situations where rapid development time, security for small and rarely used applications, and the ability of different applications to very efficiently interact, are important. Ethereum does this by building what is essentially the ultimate abstract foundational layer: a blockchain with a built-in Turing-complete programming language, allowing anyone to write smart contracts and decentralised applications where they can create their own arbitrary rules for ownership, transaction formats and state transition functions.

In 2014, Buterin and the other co-founders of Ethereum launched a crowd sourcing campaign where they sold ether to get their vision off the ground and raised more than $18 million. Each ether (ETH) sold against 0.0005 bitcoin. The first live release of Ethereum known as Frontier launched in 2015.

By late 2016, Ethereum was enabling the creation and deployment of smart contracts by third parties, making it as simple as deploying a website. Its validation time in under twelve seconds was an order-of-magnitude improvement over the bitcoin blockchain. And by implementing its programming languages — *Solidity* (Javascript like), *LLL* (Lisp-like) and *Serpent* (Python-like) — it made it easy to write smart contracts and develop dApps. Ether is mined and transferred just like bitcoins, but Ethereum is switching to a different protocol — a proof-of-stake (PoS) system as opposed to the proof-of-work (PoW) mechanism. The run-time environment of smart contracts is also called the *Ethereum Virtual Machine* (EVM). Every Ethereum node in the network runs an EVM implementation and executes the same instructions. (Readers desiring a brief explanation on what these acronyms mean can sneak peek on the chapter "Blockchain 101" at the beginning of Part II of the book).

Since Ethereum handles both crypto currency and dApps on the blockchain, it has separate accounts to manage the two. An *externally owned account* is one for users wishing to transfer ether and comes with a private key while a *contract account* has no private key and only stores the compiled bitcode of a smart contract. However, a *contract account* can collect and distribute ether, record data to the Ethereum blockchain, process information and trigger execution of other such smart contracts. Hence both account types have an ether balance.

Two other distinctions between the Bitcoin and Ethereum blockchains are notable. First, while the former allows only public or permissionless transfers, the latter allows for both permissionless and permissioned transfers. Second, Bitcoin miners which solve a new block get bitcoins as a reward. Ethereum does not offer block rewards but allows miners to take a transaction fee.

Another example of an application is a *Decentralised Autonomous Organisation* (DAO) — a programmatic organisation that runs based on rules encoded within smart contracts. So instead of the typical hierarchical structure of an organisation that is managed by humans, a decentralised organisation encodes all its rules into a smart contract and then is wholly managed by a blockchain.

Ethereum Forks and Governance

In 2016, an anonymous hacker stole US$50 million in ether in the infamous "The DAO" hack which resulted in questions about the platform's security. DAO ran an ICO on Ethereum in 2016 but had a vulnerability in its code resulting in the hack.

It caused a split within the Ethereum community regarding the return of the stolen funds. Ultimately it broke off (or forked) into two blockchains: Ethereum (ETH) and Ethereum Classic (ETC).

While in the ETH blockchain the stolen amount was reversed and restored to the original account holders, in case of ETC the immutability of the blockchain was kept sacrosanct, and the bad actors kept the stolen tokens. But Ethereum Classic hard-forked in something significant of its own — on Dec 11, 2017, Ethereum Classic implemented a fixed cap monetary policy implying that while a small stream of ether will be issued forever, classic ether will have a cap at 210 million.

The contrast between the Bitcoin blockchain and Ethereum manifests in their governance too. Bitcoin's mysterious creator never came to the forefront, and its subset of early volunteers inherited the verification rules from Satoshi Nakamoto. A few of these rules were later amended to address bugs or security vulnerabilities. But changes in Bitcoin were, and are, hard to implement owing to decentralisation in the governance itself. Ethereum's creators are a readily identifiable group who pre-mined some 70 million tokens for their ICO to raise funds and set aside another tranche of ether for founders and developers, which are now worth a staggering amount in billions of dollars. And although the founders created a not-for-profit Ethereum Foundation to manage this pool of assets, there is always the question of alignment of the interests of all stakeholders. Buterin has had much to say on the subject, some of which we discuss in our later chapter on blockchain decentralisation in Part II.

The Rise of Ether

In 2017 ether rose from just over US$8 to more than US$400, with a total market capitalisation of US$39 billion, a quarter of that of bitcoin. The price peaked at US$1291.92 on Jan 16, 2018, but currently trades at around US$200 (Sep 2018). Over 100 million ether tokens have been mined, and there is no current cap on the total number of ether that can be mined.

According to *State of the DApps* (a not-for-profit curated directory of decentralised applications on the Ethereum blockchain), there are over 1900 dApps running on Ethereum with over 11,300 active users. The *Ethereum Enterprise Alliance* (EEA), a nonprofit organisation is now over 250+ members strong and includes Fortune 500 enterprises, startups, academics and technology vendors. The Ethereum ecosystem remains one of the largest with an active developer community and active projects.

Ethereum's growth brought forth its challenges including those of scalability and security, but it has paved the way for a new paradigm of computing — one where software applications are no longer controlled by a central authority but rather operate autonomously on a decentralised, peer-to-peer network. Its intrinsic success and its ability to spawn other crypto currencies on its smart contract system for digital tokens known as ERC20 paved the way for the great ICO boom, the subject of our last chapter in Part I.

Cryptic Cryptos

March of the Altcoins

And Satoshi blessed them. And Satoshi said to them, "Be fruitful and multiply and fill the cryptosphere and subdue it, and have dominion over the fiat of governments and the gold of the heavens and over every machine and living thing that moves on the earth."

From that first bitcoin transaction in Jan 2009, what's come to pass in less than a decade is a Cambrian explosion of over 1600+ crypto currencies and counting, with a token species of every hue and colour. The Cryptic Cryptos are marching to a beat that the world is just understanding.

2017 became a landmark year for the ICO, with an explosion in "altcoin" offerings — altcoin meaning any crypto currency that's not bitcoin. As against a total value of ICOs of $268 million from 2013-Dec 2016, a total of $6.08 billion was raised in Jan-Nov 2017 alone. Of the nine biggest ICOs till then, eight of them took place in 2017:

Name	ICO Proceeds	ICO Year
Filecoin	$257 million	2017
Tezos	$236 million	2017

EOS	$200 million	2017
Paragon	$183 million	2017
The DAO	$168 million	2016
Bancor	$153 million	2017
Polkadot	$121 million	2017
QASH	$112 million	2017
Status	$109 million	2017

(Source: www.visualcapitalist.com/video-ico-explosion-one-animated-timeline)

In number terms, there were over 340 ICOs in 2017.

ICOs are set to raise much, much more in 2018 than in 2017, despite regulatory crackdowns and dire warnings from many quarters calling out a bubble in crypto currencies. Just the first three months of 2018 saw ICOs raising more money than the whole of 2017 put together. As of September 2018, more than 460 ICOs raised over $14 billion from investors seeking tokens (Source: www.coindesk.com/ico-tracker). The most significant ICOs of 2018 so far:

Name	ICO Proceeds	ICO Year
EOS	$4.1 billion	2018
Telegram	$1.7 billion	2018
Petro	$735 million	2018
Dragon Coin	$320 million	2018
Bankera	$151 million	2018

So what has caused this Cambrian explosion? While bitcoin demonstrated the success of the blockchain as a host mechanism for a crypto currency, and Ethereum followed by showing the success of blockchains in hosting distributed applications that are triggered by ether token messages, there is yet another bigger takeaway from the blockchain phenomenon — the ability to build, sustain and drive decentralised, open networks and digital communities using the blockchain tokens as incentives.

Network Effects Incentivised

To appreciate this, think about networks and what they are — they come in all shapes and sizes, like computing networks (think AWS, Azure), e-marketplaces (think Amazon, eBay), developer platforms (think GitHub), social networks (think Facebook, Instagram), company networks (a Coke or a Unilever), government networks (say the GST portal of the Indian government), university networks (edX), communications networks (think Gmail), and so on and so forth. A majority of these networks are privately owned and funded but utilise the backbone of the internet to operate.

For any network to succeed and grow, it must have a critical mass of users. The well-known network effect refers to the self-reinforcing loop that kicks in when the more existing users a network has, the more utility it offers a new user, and the more new users join in, the more its value increases for existing users in turn.

Most often, setting up a network involves raising money from sources such as venture capital funds, and then spending it on various marketing channels to attract a critical mass of users in the shortest possible time, and then letting the network effect kick-in and stimulate further growth. If the network succeeds, the benefits accrue to the people who own equity in the network.

Bitcoin as a digital currency simultaneously demonstrated the utility of a digital token in setting up and sustaining a new network from scratch, with all the attended benefits of being open and decentralised. Ethereum added the smart contracts option, allowing anyone to build a new protocol easily on top of it. And suddenly every network idea in town was fair game.

Just because the Ethereum and Bitcoin blockchains have intrinsic tokens associated with them, it doesn't mean that a protocol built on Ethereum using a smart contract must have a token associated with it, or even if it has a token, it may not be providing any financial incentive but may just represent a membership in the network or shares, etcetera.

A network has many types of participants — founders, investors, developers, end users, employees, service providers and other stakeholders. A network token that is held as a common currency by all participants in their respective capacities creates a mechanism to channelise their energies in a common direction and align their interests — that of growing the network and appreciation in the value of the token. So the founders stake is measured in token ownership, investors get tokens in return for bringing in funds, the network developers and programmers earn tokens for maintaining and growing the network, end users are rewarded for participating in the activities of the network, and even employees and service providers may be reimbursed partially or fully in tokens. The token thus rewards every network participant for their efforts and solves the bootstrap problem.

The Token Economy
Every network participant is adequately incentivised

A working example of such a network is Steemit, a blogging and social networking website built on the blockchain which uses two linked network tokens — Steem Power and Steem Dollars — to reward its users. The users are rewarded not just for posting their content but also for curating others' content through upvotes and likes and voting on comments as well. What's more, their voting strength is not uniform but a function of the Steem Power already held by them, and the earlier a person upvotes a post that becomes popular, the more is the reward. In other words, the Steemit network rewards frequent users non-linearly making it even more attractive for them to contribute their time. And by paying users half in Steem Power (a vesting token) and a half in Steem Dollars, which can be exchanged for US Dollars, Steemit has managed to add the features of a currency to its network token in addition to its utilitarian value on the content platform. When Steemit made its first significant payout to its users, it increased the value of its token, which in turn attracted new users, leading to the virtuous cycle we have been describing all along.

Initial Coin Offerings

ICOs leverage one of the most popular aspects of the power vested in network tokens — the ability to crowd source the funding required by the network to bootstrap, function and sustain its objectives. And it provides investors with an avenue to acquire network tokens and own a stake in the platform without being its actual users although they have every incentive to become participants themselves.

Though their origin has been chronicled thoroughly in the last chapter, note that in an ICO there is an advance sale of a blockchain-based project's network token mostly at the inception stage itself when the network is yet to come into existence. Mimicking the format of an IPO — the Initial Public Offering of stocks sold by companies that then get listed on a stock exchange — ICOs are predominantly unregulated activities.

Typically, a startup comes up with an idea of a network application to implement using a blockchain and proposes it to the community, sometimes by publishing a detailed white paper on it. An ICO is proposed to raise the estimated funds necessary to bring the idea to life, and aspects such as the number of network tokens that will be distributed, the price of each token and how the tokens will be used in the project's ecosystem are then decided. This is followed by marketing campaigns to gain momentum, and an ICO date is unveiled when the token sale is scheduled to begin. There is a defined period to raise the required funds after which the sale closes. Investors can pay for the new tokens through existing tokens — usually bitcoins and ether — or through fiat currencies using crypto exchanges. They receive their new tokens which in turn are listed on the crypto exchanges for trading. Many investors prefer to liquidate their new tokens for listing gains if any.

To say that ICOs have captured the imagination of the world at this moment would be an understatement. Amongst the key reasons ICOs have enjoyed so much success includes a willingness among the community to decentralise control away from large corporations, large internet firms and financial regulators. Investors are investing very early in the process, hoping to repeat the success of early stage bitcoin investors who saw its value rise astronomically creating generational wealth for some investors. Further, the surplus money people generated from early investments into crypto currencies is being re-invested into new crypto currencies. There is a genuine desire as well to fund some exciting causes and projects that are closer to the crypto-investors' hearts.

ICOs also carry a crucial benefit for the small investor in that early stage crypto-investments are not limited to private investors or Venture Capitalists (VCs). Anyone from any part of the world can take part or invest in any company that is offering their tokens for sale. It resembles the concept of Kickstarter, where people fund or support different projects which they feel would succeed and be productive, so the potential of the project plays a vital role in raising funds during an ICO. The whole ICO process is generally quite transparent all the way to completion of the fund-raising. ICOs are also easier and faster than traditional VC and Angel fund-raising, which takes at least six months for a Series A fund-raise.

The Challenges facing ICOs

While we discuss in detail the valuation and regulation conundrums facing ICOs in Part III (in the chapter "A Coin for your Thoughts"), ICOs have many challenges too. Some of these pitfalls include raising funds for the sake of raising funds, sometimes without even a minimum viable product (MVP), a development team, and clients and users. There may be the lack of a long-term vision how the project will scale with time.

It is important to check if the tokens are integral to the platform's success and if the token structure is entirely understandable. Security remains the most significant area of concern, and many projects have suffered from hacking attacks and have had the investors tokens stolen after an ICO.

ICO boom vs the Dot Com boom

The ICO hype is comparable to the Dot Com boom of the 1990s when most business plans with a website idea were being funded. The bubble eventually burst, and thousands of companies with flawed business models were purged. Those that were credible survived, creating immense value for their investors, and included names like Google, Amazon and eBay. ICO investors today should challenge themselves to find the next

Bitcoin or Google amongst the upcoming flurry of ICOs by identifying sustainable and scalable businesses.

There is a lot of debate whether ICOs are any different from VC or Angel funding. ICOs are a new way of raising funds for good business ideas like any other form of investment. VCs arguably bring more value with their teams' experience and a network of contacts besides the money they invest. Either way, there will always be space for Angel investors, VCs, crowd-funding platforms and ICOs to co-exist with each other.

Fork a Token

We saw that the mechanism for creating tokens is flexible and can represent lots of different things — from paid credits or membership within the decentralised application to an entitlement to a share of profits, ownership interest in the protocol, voting power in the company, or just a digital asset that can be freely traded on crypto currency exchanges.

While ICOs raise money by selling new tokens, forking is an equally popular alternative, since forks typically sprout from bitcoins riding on its fame. Current bitcoin owners may become eligible for the forked coin, providing the new token with an upfront user base. And of course, it helps to have the forked token named after bitcoin in some way or the other. Miners have a vested interest in helping create the new forked tokens for their rewards. Some forks only fork code without continuing the same blockchain. For example, Litecoin is a fork of Bitcoin's code, but owners of bitcoins didn't receive free litecoins when the Litecoin network launched. Tokens like ZCash and Monero have also forked the Bitcoin blockchain and built their tokens on top. Bitcoin Cash, which hard-forked from the Bitcoin blockchain on Aug 1, 2017, with a key change of increasing the blocksize parameter by eight times, is now the fourth most valuable coin according to CoinMarketCap.

Tokens like Gnosis and Augur are built on top of the Ethereum blockchain apart from its native Ether. The underlying blockchain provides an immutable record of the entire holding and transfer of the crypto currencies built on top of it, serving a similar function to what central banks do in the case of physical currencies like the USD.

Some coins (tokens) are pegged to another stable asset, like gold or the U.S. dollar, and are called "stable coins". It allows for a drastic reduction in the volatility of the coin's value, making it easier to use for day-to-day transactions. Examples include MakerDao, Tether and Basecoin, all of which peg themselves to the US dollar.

Ethereum has emerged as the platform of choice for tokenised networks and projects, with 94 out of the top 100 blockchain projects launched on it. It has also spawned the most significant number of ICOs, thanks to its ERC20 smart contract system which allows new tokens to exist without their blockchain or mining community, depending on Ethereum for the same. It has also made ether as the currency of choice over bitcoins for a new ICO.

This saga helps us to conclude Part I of this book, and in Part II, we put under the lens four crucial aspects of a blockchain to complete our understanding of the strengths and weaknesses of this fantastic new technology.

Part II

Blockchain 101

The Essential Lexicon

> The acronym CRUD — Create Read Update Delete — describes traditional data management. Blockchain is CRU. There's no delete.
> — Jon Brock

Before we critique the different aspects of the blockchain technology, for readers who may be unfamiliar with its constituent technologies and technical terms, this chapter will provide a quick introduction.

Bitcoin and Ethereum — the most famous use cases — will be used to illustrate the concepts.

Blockchain

A blockchain is defined as an immutable, sequential chain of records called *Blocks*. The records can contain transactions, files or any other data, and are chained together using *hashes*. It is implemented and managed by a peer-to-peer network of computers (also known as *peers* or *nodes*) spread all over the globe.

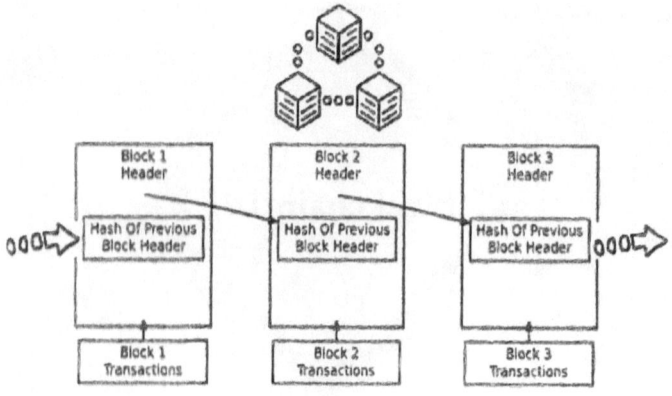

Blockchain
Schematic Diagram

Each node stores a copy (or a nearly exact copy) of the entire blockchain and coordinates with other nodes using software protocols. Replicating data in this way makes the blockchain remarkably resilient to corruption or network failure, for as long as a single consistent copy of the blockchain exists on a single node anywhere in the world, the entire network can be seeded again for new transactions.

The software protocol to record new data in any blockchain is called a *consensus mechanism*, which is necessarily a set of rules coupled with economic incentives and costs, making it difficult and costly for any one node to unilaterally modify data stored on the blockchain. The consensus mechanism enables a blockchain-based network to periodically reach an agreement on the current state of the shared database even if the members do not know or trust one another.

Public-private key cryptography is used to validate the integrity of the data on the blockchain and the people engaging in the transaction need not reveal their true identities. Hence on a publicly accessible blockchain anyone can create an account comprising a public address and a private key and engage in transactions with others without the intervention of any third-party.

Bitcoin Blockchain

The first blockchain that was built using the principles described by its originator Satoshi Nakamoto in his famous white paper — *Bitcoin: A Peer-to-Peer Electronic Cash System.*

Bitcoin (the crypto currency)

The digital token on the Bitcoin blockchain that is mined and used as a crypto currency. Bitcoin has demonstrated that using a blockchain anyone can freely exchange digital currencies without a central clearinghouse and without disclosing their identities. Ever since its launch in 2009, Bitcoin has become one of the largest payment systems in the world.

Public-Private Key Encryption

In the early days of the internet, sending private messages was difficult. To send an encrypted message, it would be scrambled using a key (also called cypher), and then decoded by the recipient using the same key. The key had to be agreed upon before exchanging the messages and had to be separately communicated to the recipient before the message itself. Hence if a key were compromised, the encryption stood defeated.

Public-private key encryption overcame this problem by eliminating the need for a shared key, but by using a pair of keys — a widely disseminated public key and a private key. The party sending the message can encrypt it using the receiver's public key, which can then only be decrypted by the receiver using the private key.

In 1978, a team of cryptographers in MIT developed the RSA algorithm to create a mathematically linked set of public and private keys generated by multiplying together two large prime numbers, since while multiplying them is easy, it is exceptionally difficult to prime factorise the result in reverse. The RSA algorithm enabled people to broadcast their public keys widely, knowing that it would be nearly impossible to uncover the underlying private keys. This then further led to the development of the concept of digital signatures.

Bitcoin relies on public-private key cryptography for people to create their bitcoin accounts under a digital alias without seeking anyone's permission.

Having created an account, people can then send bitcoins to anyone in the world by executing and signing digitally a transaction with a private key. Members (or nodes) of the network then verify that the transaction is valid and update the balances of the corresponding bitcoin accounts by recording them in the blockchain using the bitcoin protocol — a free and open-source software.

Cryptographic Hash

A hash function takes an input value (any data - numbers, files, etcetera) and creates an output value deterministic of the input value. For any x input value, you will always receive the same $y = f(x)$ output value whenever the hash function f runs. In this way, every input has a determined output. For example, the hash function md5 creates a 32 character hexadecimal output from any input data:

md5("hello world") = 5eb63bbbe01eeed093cb22bb8f5acdc3

Hash functions are generally irreversible (one-way), which means you can't figure out the input if you only know the output

– unless you try every possible input (called a brute-force attack). Hash functions are often used for proving that something is the same as something else, without revealing the information beforehand.

In case of a blockchain, every new block added to the blockchain database contains a hash (cryptographic hash) of the previous block which makes it tamper-resistant. This is because changing any particular transaction in the blockchain database would change the hash of the block being tampered with, which would cascade to all the subsequent blocks added in the blockchain.

Nodes

A node can be a computer or some other network device like a printer which has a unique network address to permit the exchange of data. Hence the nodes can create, receive, store or send data along the network routes.

Peer-to-peer (P2P)

P2P implies that there is no central point in the system or network, all nodes act in conjunction with each other to collectively achieve the output.

In other words, each node can act as a server for the others to allow sharing of data without the need for a central server. All peers are equally privileged.

Block Header

The core of a block's header is a unique fingerprint or hash of all the transactions contained in that block, along with a timestamp and a hash of the previous block.

Block

Sets of transactions are grouped together into blocks which are then linked together in a sequential time-stamped chain using information in the respective block headers. The entire chain of blocks is then referred to as the blockchain.

In case of the bitcoin blockchain, each block stores all the information about transfers of bitcoins from one account to another.

Protocol (or Protocol Layer)

The protocol is that set of special rules that nodes in a blockchain network use when they transmit or receive information, and by which consensus is maintained across the network. A similar example would be the TCP/IP protocol which forms the backbone of communication on the internet itself.

Proof-of-Work (PoW)

A Proof-of-Work algorithm (PoW) is how new Blocks are created or mined on the blockchain. The goal of PoW is to discover a number which is the solution to a mathematical problem. The number must be computationally difficult to find but easy to verify by anyone on the network. This is the core idea behind Proof of Work.

In case of the Bitcoin blockchain, while generating a hash for any given block need not be challenging, the bitcoin protocol purposefully makes this task difficult by requiring that a block's hash begin with a specified number of leading zeroes, which constitutes the PoW. Any computer trying to generate a valid hash must run through repeated calculations to meet the protocol's stringent requirements.

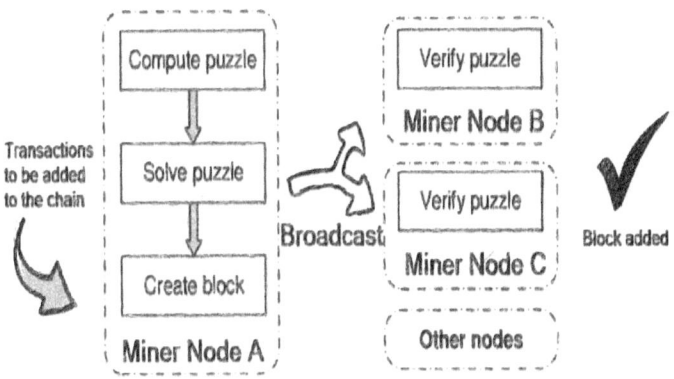

Proof-of-Work
Schematic Diagram

Ultimately, the bitcoin protocol creates what can be regarded as a "state transition system". Every ten minutes, the bitcoin network updates its "state", calculating the balances of all existing bitcoin accounts. The PoW consensus algorithm serves as a "state transition function" that takes the current state of the bitcoin network and updates it with a new set of bitcoin transactions. Even though bitcoin lacks a central clearinghouse, users gain assurance that the balance of every bitcoin account is accurate at any given time. The protocol enables trusted peer-to-peer transactions between people who do not know and hence may not trust, one another. That is why blockchain technology is called a *trustless* system.

Miners

The nodes which carry out the intensive PoW computations and solve the mathematical puzzle required for them to generate the hash needed to add a new block on the blockchain are usually referred to as Miners. The bitcoin protocol adjusts the difficulty of the mathematical puzzle depending on the number of miners on the bitcoin network participating in the PoW game to ensure that a new block gets added approximately every ten minutes. The more the number of miners, the harder it becomes to generate a valid hash with an appropriate number of leading zeroes.

Having arrived at a valid hash, the miner then broadcasts the same to the rest of the network which re-verify it using a simple calculation at their end, and then add the block to their local blockchain copies.

Consensus Mechanism and Soft Forks

The bitcoin protocol incorporates a consensus mechanism that helps members of the network agree whether a bitcoin transaction is valid and should be recorded in the blockchain, and who owns what amount of bitcoins at any given point in time. Occasionally, the bitcoin network soft forks, or splits into multiple copies, when different portions of the network append a different block to the blockchain. This could happen for different reasons, for example, when an updated version of the client running the bitcoin network is released and a number of nodes connected to the network fail to update their software.

When the bitcoin blockchain soft forks, the database structure turns into a tree rather than a linear chain. To ensure that the network converges towards the same branch of the tree, the bitcoin protocol implements a fork rule stipulating that in case of a fork, miners should always pick the longest chain — that is, the branch with the most confirmed blocks as measured by computational power required to validate these blocks. This rule enables the bitcoin protocol to preserve consensus throughout the network. If a majority of the network agrees on a particular chain of transactions that chain is presumed valid. Bitcoin holders thus trust that at any given time those controlling a majority of the computational power supporting the bitcoin network are acting in accordance with the protocol's rules, verifying transactions and recording new blocks to the longest chain.

Tokens - Incentives for Mining

To compensate for the cost of engaging in bitcoin mining, the bitcoin protocol implements an incentivisation scheme to encourage people to maintain the bitcoin chain. Every time a miner generates a valid hash for a new block of transactions, the bitcoin network will credit the miner's account with a specific amount of a digital native token or bitcoin — known as *block reward* — along with transaction fees. Miners on the bitcoin network thus have an economic incentive to validate transactions and engage in the PoW guessing game.

Because the Bitcoin protocol is only programmed to allocate 21 million bitcoins, the block reward program progressively decreases over time — halving once every approximately four years from its launch in January 2009 until approximately 2140. Tokens such as bitcoins thus represent digital assets which have ownership and are transferable.

In general, tokens are digital assets which can be owned and transferred. They can be native tokens of a blockchain like bitcoins and ether, or tokens of blockchains forked from Bitcoin or Ethereum or others (BitCash, Monrero), or tokens created on a new protocol implemented on top of existing blockchains like Bitcoin and Ethereum (Augur, Gnosis).

Initial Coin Offering (ICO)

The process by which blockchain startups offer investors units of a new digital token or crypto currency in exchange for crypto currencies like bitcoin or ether. First held in 2013, this method became the rage in 2017 and accelerated in 2018 as the primary way to fund the development of new crypto currencies. The pre-created tokens are then sold and traded on crypto currency exchanges if there is a demand for them.

Crypto Exchanges

A crypto exchange allows its clients to trade their crypto currencies with each other or in exchange with regular fiat currencies.

The crypto exchanges set the exchange rates for the various token and currencies based on the actions of their sellers and buyers as well as on the wider market rates on other exchanges as well.

However, there can be other factors affecting the price on a particular exchange, since there is no regulatory oversight at all. Exchanges charge a commission on intra-crypto trades and typically a higher fee on crypto-fiat exchanges.

Crypto exchanges can be either centralised or decentralised. Generally, fiat-to-crypto currency exchanges tend to be more centralised because they integrate with the traditional financial system, whereas crypto-to-crypto wallets are decentralised where the customer controls their own funds, a point explained in detail in the next chapter.

Crypto Wallets (Hot and Cold)

A crypto currency wallet is a software program that stores private and public keys and interacts with various blockchains to enable the user to transact with different digital currencies. The wallet software has embedded commands that allow these transactions with each crypto currency having its own unique address and commands.

A Hot Wallet holds the private and public keys in storage even as it remains connected to the internet. Hence these are always susceptible to cyber-attacks or theft. Hot wallets are software programs which can be computer-based, mobile-based or cloud-based.

A Cold Wallet, on the other hand, is much more secure as it stores the keys offline. It is only when the user wishes to transact with those currencies that the wallet needs to be connected to the internet. These can be independent hardware devices with robust security features which need to be put online through a computer when transacting.

Ethereum

The second-generation public blockchain that, unlike the Bitcoin blockchain, focuses on running decentralised programs called Smart Contracts. Miners work to earn *ether*, the crypto currency token that fuels the network and used by application developers to pay for transaction fees and services on the Ethereum network.

There is a second type of token that is used to pay miners fees for including transactions in their block, called *gas*, and every smart contract execution requires a certain amount of gas to be sent along with it to entice miners to put it in the blockchain.

Application Layer

The topmost layer of the blockchain network where a distributed application resides and executes. Bitcoin's scripting language enables us to write a script that is recorded with each transaction, allowing us to encode rules to communicate on the blockchain and build applications. Similarly, Ethereum has the *Ethereum Virtual Machines* (EVM) and its own scripting languages to code applications called Smart Contracts on the blockchain. Hence the complete stack may be viewed as:

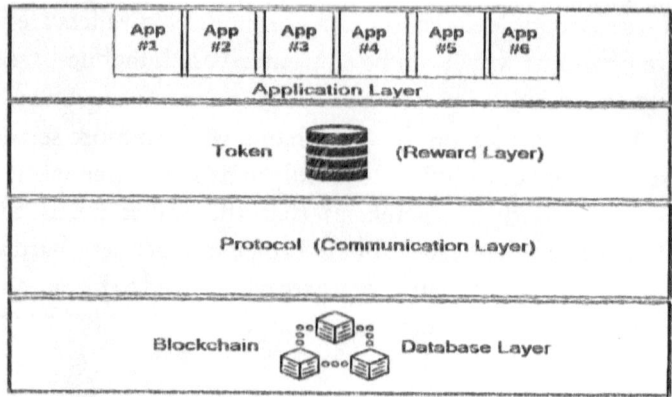

EVM Stack
Schematic Diagram

Ethereum Virtual Machine (EVM)

The Ethereum protocol processes transactions and smart contracts using what is called the Ethereum Virtual Machine (EVM). Every node that is participating in the Ethereum network runs the EVM, and hence it is computationally intensive. To compensate for this, and to incentivise the nodes (or miners), the protocol allows the miners to charges a small fee referred to as *gas*.

Transactions originate from *externally-owned accounts* whereas *messages* originate from *contract accounts*. Both *transactions* and *messages* are objects containing a particular quantity of ether, an array of data, the address of the sender, and a destination address. For *transactions* the destination address can be either another *contract account* or an *externally-owned account* whereas for a *message* it can only be another *contract account*. Hence *messages* allow *contracts* to call one another.

Anyone can trigger the execution of a smart contract by sending an ether transaction to the corresponding *contract account*. When a *contract* receives a *message*, it has the option of returning a *message* to the original sender just like a standard computer function.

The price of gas is not fixed but is dynamically adjusted by miners based on the market price of ether. Because all active nodes on Ethereum run the code of every smart contract, the code is not controlled by—and cannot be halted by—any single party.

A smart contract thus operates as an autonomous agent, automatically reacting to inputs received from externally-owned accounts or other smart contract programs executed on the network.

Proof-of-Stake (PoS)

Proof-of-stake is an alternative process for transaction verification on a blockchain. Unlike the PoW system, in which the user validates transactions and creates new blocks by performing a certain amount of computational work, a PoS system requires the user to show ownership of a certain number of crypto currency tokens. Blocks are not "mined". In most cases, a fixed number of tokens are created at launch and transaction fees is paid for adding blocks.

In order to validate transactions and create blocks, validating nodes must first put their own tokens at 'stake'. If they validate a fraudulent transaction, they lose their token holdings, as well as their rights to participate in the future. Once the stake is put up, nodes can partake in the process, and because they have staked their own money, they are incentivised to validate the right transactions.

This system does not provide a way to handle the initial distribution of coins at the founding phase of the crypto currency, so crypto currencies which use this system either begin with an ICO and sell their pre-mined coins, or begin with the PoW system, and switch over to the PoS system later.

Delegated Proof-of-Stake (DPoS)

In a Delegated Proof-of-stake process for transaction verification on a blockchain, all nodes vote to elect a limited number of nodes who they trust to validate transactions on their behalf. This speeds up the consensus mechanism without sacrificing decentralisation. The voting is an ongoing process, and the elected nodes can be replaced any time the others deem them untrustworthy. Like in the PoS processes, loss of income and reputation act as incentives against malicious behaviour.

ERC20 Token Standard

Ethereum can be used as a platform to launch other crypto currencies on the back of its ERC20 token standard. Other developers can issue their own versions of this token and raise funds though ICOs.

ERC721 Token Standard

Ethereum has also created the ERC721 token standard for tracking unique digital assets, such as digital collectables, and allows people to prove ownership of scarce digital goods.

Decentralised Autonomous Organisations (DAOs)

Ethereum can also be used to build Decentralised Autonomous Organisations (DAO). A DAO is a fully autonomous, decentralised organisation with no single leader. DAOs' are run on a collection of smart contracts written on the Ethereum blockchain.

The code is designed to replace the rules and structure of a traditional organisation, eliminating the need for people and centralised control. A DAO is owned by everyone who purchases tokens, but instead of each token equating to equity shares and ownership, tokens act as contributions that give people voting rights.

Distributed Ledger Technologies

Distributed ledger technology uses independent computers (nodes) to record, share and synchronise transactions in their respective electronic ledgers, instead of keeping data centralised on a server as in a traditional ledger. The blockchain is one example of this technology.

Having completed a quick review of some important terms and concepts, we begin our critique of the blockchain technology by picking its first core feature — decentralisation, sometimes referred to as "peer-to-peer".

De.cen.tra.lis.ed

By Netizens, For Netizens, Of Netizens

Blockchain Technology may offer a way to re-decentralise the internet: Startups want to remake the internet with blockchain
— The headline of a Special Report article in
The Economist, Jun 30th, 2018.

Who owns the internet?

A simple enough question, you might say, why not just google it? And Google answers — no one. The catch, of course, lies in the verb "google".

For billions of people, the internet only means using one or more of the FAANG applications and their ilk — the FAANGs being Facebook, Amazon, Apple, Netflix and Google. From the perspective of such people, the FAANGs own the internet, and the decentralised internet backbone is invisible to them. Even in the highly-walled online world in China (pun intended), there are the FAANG counterparts called BAT — Baidu, Alibaba, Tencent — who, along with Xiaomi and Ant Financial, dominate the applications space and the user experience in that country.

This dichotomy between the architecture of the Internet (Web 1.0), which is decentralised, versus the (social) applications dominating it (Web 2.0), creating such massive networks of centralisation, appeared organically over time. Theoretically, on the internet, every individual user has an independent voice, access to the same tools as the big-guys and equal reach to any corner of the world. Practically, the FAANGs determine what we see, mould our opinions in subtle ways, filter our voice and set the narrative.

Their ability to use our data against us is the source of their power, and network effect guarantees them of an ever-increasing flow of such data for free as more users get locked-in. Advertisers pay richly to access this data, and even with the current backlash against misuse and privacy violations, the scene has hardly altered. The Facebook-Cambridge Analytica saga is just one major instance in this huge arena of ongoing debates and its transforming impact on people as a whole, a subject on which reams are being written, but is beyond the scope of this book.

Our scope here is to examine if the decentralised nature of blockchains and the distributed applications (dApps) executing on them are game-changers in any way leading to the foundation of Web 3.0. A model scenario would be one in which the user data is de-linked from the dApps themselves, and where the dApps may have to pay users in crypto currency to access their data and users may pay the dApps for using their services. The users are empowered and in control of their data and privacy at all times.

The implicit assumption is that decentralised, or "peer-to-peer", is better than centralised, not only in the scenario painted above but also because decentralised is robust (being both fault-tolerant and attack-resistant) while centralised will have a single point of failure, and because decentralised is collusion-resistant while centralised is prone to manipulation.

To get a handle on the various aspects of decentralisation in the context of blockchains and crypto currencies, here is Vitalik Buterin, the man behind Ethereum, himself writing on *The Meaning of Decentralisation* (Medium, Feb 6, 2017):

> "Decentralisation" is one of the words that is used in the crypto economics space the most frequently, and is often even viewed as a blockchain's entire raison d'être, but it is also one of the words that is perhaps defined the most poorly. Thousands of hours of research, and billions of dollars of hashpower, have been spent for the sole purpose of attempting to achieve decentralisation, and to protect and improve it, and when discussions get rivalrous it is extremely common for proponents of one protocol (or protocol extension) to claim that the opposing proposals are "centralised" as the ultimate knockdown argument.

Decentralisation in Ethereum — Buterin's View

Buterin draws a subtle distinction between being "decentralised" and "distributed", and how this plays out at three different layers in any system, which he calls the Architectural layer, the Political layer and the Logical layer. At the Architectural layer, decentralisation is about how many physical computers comprise the system, and how robust is it against hardware failures of any sort. Political decentralisation deals with how many individuals or organisations control the computers that comprise the system, while Logical decentralisation talks about the external interface of the system — is it a single monolithic object or an amorphous swarm, that is, if the system was cut in half, including its providers and users, will both halves continue to operate independently? He then concludes that:

> Blockchains are politically decentralised (no one controls them) and architecturally decentralised (no infrastructural

central point of failure) but they are logically centralised (there is one commonly agreed state and the system behaves like a single computer).

It is usually suggested that Bitcoin is truly decentralised — there is no central point of failure. There is no dependence on one person, one node, one company, one nation, or one leader. But deeper delves from the history of Bitcoin and Ethereum are instructive.

In 2016, the DAO Hack resulted in Buterin's Ethereum network going through one of the most prominent hard forks in the history of crypto currencies. The DAO project was a transaction system built on top of the Ethereum blockchain, and a bug in it allowed a hacker to move 3.6 million Ether (ETH) within hours. Since Ethereum did not support a soft fork, the only option for saving the lost Ether and going back to normal was to split the blockchain, that is, a hard fork which would deny the DAO hack and return Ether to the investors. This was voted upon, and with 89% in favour, it was implemented on July 20, 2016, with the Ethereum blockchain splitting at block number 1,920,000. The rest of the community split off to support the old immutable chain giving birth to a new token — Ethereum Classic (ETC).

The point of bringing up the story of the DAO hack and the consequent Ethereum hard fork is that it is a direct indicator of how centralised Ether is. While a nimble response in a crisis is a huge positive, as is the ability to safeguard investor interest, it is only possible with high centralisation and control.

But for a token acting as a currency and thus acting as a storehouse of value, this is an inherent contradiction. The possibility of a hard fork undermines the stability and immutability of a currency. It is akin to a central bank's control over fiat currency. This is how Buterin himself put it in his post cited above:

However, this presents a fundamental paradox. Many communities, including Ethereum's, are often praised for having a strong community spirit and being able to coordinate quickly on implementing, releasing and activating a hard fork to fix denial-of-service issues in the protocol within six days. But how can we foster and improve this good kind of coordination, but at the same time prevent "bad coordination" that consists of miners trying to screw everyone else over by repeatedly coordinating 51% attacks?

Bitcoin versus the Altcoins

Bitcoin has also suffered similar hard forks in its history in Aug 2010 and Aug 2017 — the former to compensate for a security breach and latter on technical grounds (change of the block size). Jimmy Song in *Why Bitcoin is Different* (Medium, Apr 2, 2018) claims that every crypto currency and ICO other than bitcoin is centralised. His argument stems from the fact that in any ICO the entity that pre-mines the initial tokens is by default the centralised party which retains the right to change the token's usage or incentives and issue additional tokens.

Further, he claims that Altcoins are no different from fiat currencies issued by any government because like them the current and future Altcoin leaders may tax or inflate away the value of the coins or even confiscate them. Ethereum qualifies as a centrally-controlled currency as it has had at least five hard forks where users were forced to upgrade, some poor decisions were bailed out, and there is some talk of a new storage tax. Buterin has said as much.

In contrast, it is Satoshi's disappearing act that made all the difference in bitcoin's case where multiple parties have some say in how the network is run, upgrades are voluntary, there is no single point of failure, their scarcity is real instead of theoretical, and an owner of bitcoins has full sovereign control on them, which makes it a good store of value.

We dwell more on the combined effect of such contradictions in our subsequent chapters culminating in The Scalability Trilemma.

Measuring Decentralisation

Can a blockchain's decentralisation property be quantified and measured in any sense? Balaji S. Srinivasan (CTO, Coinbase) and Leland Lee make such an attempt in their post *Quantifying Decentralisation* (Medium, Jul 28, 2017) by proposing what they call the *Minimum Nakamoto coefficient,* basing it on similarities to the Gini Coefficient and Lorenz Curve used to measure income inequality in a population.

An interesting insight from their work lies in the distinction they create between a decentralised system and its decentralised subsystems, a different classification from Buterin's three layers model discussed above.

For instance, they divide the Bitcoin system into six subsystems — Mining (by reward), Client (by codebase), Developers (by commits), Exchanges (by volume), Nodes (by country) and Ownership (by addresses) — and then postulate that if any "essential" sub-system (say mining) is centralised, then the whole system may be treated as centralised. One subsystem makes the whole vulnerable.

To quantify and compare aspects of Bitcoin and Ethereum Decentralisation, they calculate the Lorenz curves and Gini coefficients for each of the six Bitcoin and Ethereum subsystems and are then able to draw some conclusions such as that in Ethereum mining and development are more centralised than Bitcoin, while client centralisation is roughly equal in both instances.

But it is this observation of theirs that bears some mulling — it appears that a very high level of wealth centralisation is still compatible with the operation of a decentralised protocol.

That brings us right back to the opening remarks of this chapter — just as the FAANG apps resulted in the centralisation of data even while running on a decentralised backbone, the blockchain serving as a similar decentralised ledger-backbone cannot prevent the centralisation of wealth. The 1% continue their reign uninhibited.

Centralisation in the Exchanges

Srinivasan does not mention if he considers exchanges to be one of the "essential" sub-systems, but crypto exchanges function in a most centralised manner. Brian Armstrong, CEO of Coinbase, one of the largest crypto exchanges in *Is Coinbase creating a centralised or decentralised financial system?* (Medium, May 2, 2018) tackles this question head-on and confesses as much:

> An employee asked me recently how we're creating an open financial system if we're a centralised company.
> It's a good question and here was my answer.
> People need to be able to do both of the following:
> 1. Get access to crypto currency — this tends to be more centralised
> 2. Use crypto currency — this tends to be more decentralised
> Coinbase has products in both of these areas, and the first one helps the second one happen.
> Allow me to explain…
> Adoption of crypto currency will happen in several phases.
> In the investment phase people speculate and try to make money on crypto. This is where 90% of activity is happening today, primarily via centralised exchanges.
> In the utility phase people begin using crypto as a payment network, transacting for real goods and services, interacting with dapps, etc. This is where about 10% of the total activity is happening today, primarily via decentralised (user-

controlled) wallets.

In other words, the investment phase draws enough people in that a critical mass of people is reached to spark the utility phase, or come for the tool, stay for the network.

Fiat-to-crypto exchanges tend to be more centralised because they integrate with the traditional financial system. For example, Coinbase and GDAX make it easy to connect your bank account and buy crypto. This means we work closely with banks and regulators to build the most compliant systems. There is a lot of interaction with the "real world" in each country to make this work.

Crypto-to-crypto wallets, by contrast, are more decentralised. The customer controls their own funds. For example, Toshi and Coinbase Commerce use a user-controlled wallet.

There are exceptions to each of the above. For example, decentralised exchanges, and centralised wallets both offer compelling advantages, even if they are less popular today.

The overall point is that there will be both centralised and decentralised products which help create an open financial system, just like ISPs (centralised) and browsers (decentralised) both play a key role in the internet ecosystem. It's a false dichotomy to pit one against the other because both are a part of the solution.

Decentralised dApps

Having examined some ground realities of decentralisation in the context of crypto currencies, let us turn our attention to the other big blockchain promise — dApps.

While proven dApps are few and far between, promising stories have emerged. In the decentralised file-and-data storage space, for example, there are projects like Storj and Inter-Planetary File System (IPFS) which are gaining significant traction, and we examine their models briefly to demonstrate decentralisation at its best.

Storj is the open-source, decentralised, blockchain-based counterpart of Dropbox, OneDrive, S3 and Google Drive. Storj nodes, or average computers running the software, sell resources to store and transfer information and earn STORJ (or other crypto currencies) in exchange for their services. STORJ digital tokens are based on the Ethereum blockchain. All files that are uploaded and stored are encrypted, and only the owner of the files has the encryption keys. Each encrypted file is split into shards and distributed to different nodes throughout the network, all shards are also mirrored a few times to other nodes in the network, and unless every single node goes down, which is near impossible, there will never be downtime.

IPFS has emerged from the work of Juan Benet. ConsenSys (Medium, Jun 30, 2016) describes it as the "Lego kit for the third web" where, instead of a central server, a peer-to-peer network is used to establish connections, and Public key cryptography is built into the node addressing system and content addressing is used to index content. Both node and content addresses are stored in a decentralised naming system called IPNS. Nodes in the peer-to-peer network each hold private keys and release public keys, just like in Bitcoin or Ethereum, thus incorporating security in the addressing system itself. A content address is derived by hashing a piece of content and then hashed again to derive a key name which in turn is associated with a human-readable name in IPNS (IPFS' address registry). Because IPFS addresses are derived from the content they refer to, if the content still exists anywhere on the network, links will always resolve. A Filecoin token is being developed to incentivise the storage and serving of content.

Some other dApps that might deserve mention are OpenBazaar, an alternative to the traditional e-commerce set-up, and CryptoKitties in the gaming space, which is a marketplace for unique digital pets on the Ethereum blockchain.

Steemit rewards its million-strong community for posting and rating content with their digital tokens — "Steem Power" and "Steem Dollars". Steem Dollars can be encashed through exchanges thus making it liquid and attractive to its users while Steem Power is less convertible but increases the voting power of their owners in the community. The other side of this coin is that 90% of Steem Power is held by 2% of the users, bringing back the perils of concentration.

Decentralised Smart Contracts

There happens to be a theoretical limitation to designing the perfect smart contract residing on the blockchain that guarantees flawless execution each time it is invoked. The limitation stems from the fact that no contract writer can anticipate every single outcome under a given set of contract conditions.

Professor Oliver Hart of Harvard, who has won a Nobel prize for his work on contract theory, has stated in his "Incomplete Theory of Contracts" that contracts are always incomplete, and just as we cannot predict the future, we cannot anticipate all possible contract outcomes. Hence expecting an algorithm to compensate for a theoretical impossibility is absurd. Human judgment will have to be exercised in cases, howsoever far and few, where the smart contract fails to execute under stipulated conditions, hence perfect decentralisation in the case of smart contracts cannot be achieved either. It seems it is impossible to take the human out of the blockchain, and that makes the blockchain that much more fallible and fragile.

Hence, the overall picture that emerges is that a decentralised Web 3.0 still lies in the future. Satoshi Nakamoto's sacrifice in giving up control of the Bitcoin blockchain certainly proved what is possible, but that's exactly where things stand today after a decade. That the urge for decentralisation manifests itself very profoundly can be judged by just one man's yeoman efforts in this direction.

Sir Tim Berners-Lee, the inventor of the World-Wide-Web — sometimes called the "Father of the Web" — has, for some years now, devoted himself to working on decentralising the Internet with an open-source project called *Solid*, the sole aim being to put the power of user data back in the hands of the users themselves. *Solid* is derived from the term "social linked data" and does not use the blockchain. Speaking at the Decentralised Web Summit in San Francisco in 2016, he said the decentralised and free ethos that underpins the internet will prevail:

> "You can make the walled garden very, very sweet," he said. "But the jungle outside is always more appealing in the long term."

In light of the opening quote from The Economist Special Report at the beginning of this chapter, suffice to say that even "re-decentralisation" is embedded and cannot be free from "centralisation"!

Trust from Trustless

Consensus Begets Trust and Truth

> The root problem with conventional currency is all the trust that's required to make it work. The central bank must be trusted not to debase the currency, but the history of fiat currencies is full of breaches of that trust.
> — Satoshi Nakamoto, inventor of Blockchain and Bitcoin

> And that brings us to tonight's word: Truthiness. Now I'm sure some of the word-police, the "wordanistas" over at Websters, are gonna say, "Hey, that's not a word!" Well, anybody who knows me knows that I am no fan of dictionaries or reference books. They're elitist. Constantly telling us what is or isn't true, what did or didn't happen…
> — Stephen Colbert, comedian and the host of *The Colbert Report*

When our ancestors roamed the jungle as hunter-gatherers, trust in a fellow human was sometimes forged in the face of a sabre-toothed tiger or against the harsh elements of nature. Trust within the tribe and the sharing of food and shelter guaranteed survival in the world's ab initio peer-to-peer network. Consensus within the tribe members was very much the basis of both trust and truth, and we had earlier cited the example of the Yapese people who operated the first primitive blockchain on these principles.

The transition to agriculture gave birth to *Homo Economicus*. Agriculture surplus could be stored and traded with barter being the simplest exchange. It led to the measurement of economic value, specialisation of occupations and the development of currencies, markets and finance. Along with this arose property rights, questions of common good, trust and dispute resolution. It led to the creation of states and monarchies and enshrined taxation, warfare and governance in the human ecosystem.

Centuries of economic evolution coupled with technological progress have culminated in our current mix of Capitalism dominating the world, despite regressive tendencies like increasing economic inequality and the market dominance and distortions of hegemonic firms.

While the economic and political history is too vast to capture in a few paragraphs, the steady increase in economic complexity brought challenges related to trust in the system. In any economic system, there will always be bad actors willing to disrupt it or exploit it, and solutions to combat mala fide actions have verged on a judicious mix of regulation and centralised control. Everything needs to be regulated to a degree — from markets to currencies and from stock exchanges to banks.

Centralisation makes regulation easier but engenders friction as compliance and reporting costs kick in, and transactions slow down as they pass through an audit and approval chain. For example, in India, all banks are directly regulated by the Reserve Bank of India, which also has the mandate to control the printing of currency, management of money supply and foreign exchange reserves of the country. The flip side of centralisation is that it also becomes a single point of failure, so when the regulator fails to act, the results are usually catastrophic. Trust implies vulnerability.

Regulation and centralised control have been implemented in varied ways, with powers vesting in designated corporations, voluntary bodies, trade associations, governments and sovereign institutions. Even in international institutions that have been created just for the purpose.

The single reason to build this elaborate network of regulators and intermediaries remains — Trust. Often, trust engenders the truth, for the truth is easiest to arrive at when facts emanate from a trusted source. It enables parties who have never transacted with each other to conclude deals and transactions successfully by placing their trust in known regulators, institutions and intermediaries — sometimes for a fee — to record the truth of the transactions being concluded or the assets being transferred.

The power of branding can be counted upon to enhance the degree of trust manifold along with the fee commanded. So a US Federal Reserve commands the respect that makes the US Dollar the reserve currency of the world even though it is just a fiat currency like any other currency in the world. A Paypal commands a disproportionate share of the online payments market just as a Western Union does for physical remittances of money. Credit card payments are practically split between Mastercard and Visa. While not immune from fraud and blow-ups, the current system has worked well for global economic growth and commerce.

Trust in the Platform, not in the Institution

Technology, however, like the proverbial joker in the pack, has been disrupting the old order. Platforms like Uber and Airbnb heralded the "sharing economy". They made it easy to share a ride with unknown people or sleep in a stranger's house without a second thought because you could trust the crowd-sourced ratings of these apps. Trust evolved, and technology-driven crowdsourced platforms enabled a new economy to emerge — the app-driven gig economy.

The apps continued innovating and soon ratings became a bi-directional phenomenon. So when you hail a ride, not only do you rate the driver on comfort, skill and courtesy, but the reverse is true as well — passengers are rated for their behaviour by the drivers.

The sharing economy depends on mutual accountability, and ratings are at its very core. Algorithms can then decide who qualifies as highly trustworthy with a "5-star" rating, and whom not to trust because of consistently low ratings, irrespective of the which side of the transaction is involved — service provider or consumer. It becomes so easy to weed out the "difficult" customer or supplier and deny them their existence on the platform for lack of trust.

It is not as if these innovations do not bring along their own unique set of flaws. Subjectivity is rife in any rating activity and cannot be free from racist, casteist and sexist impulses. Rachel Botsman in her recent book *Who Can You Trust* (2017) emphasises that the distribution of trust through technology impacts our behaviour in the real world in both positive and negative ways, making us accountable in ways we cannot even imagine yet. A rating culture also puts us in competition with each other, with an "Uber Rating" becoming a flaunting point on the social media. China, which has taken the concept of a "social score" to a whole new level, aims to have every citizens' ratings on a database.

That there remains a significant point of centralisation, which is the platform or app itself, causes yet more distortions in the rating system and the way trust is engendered by the platform. The algorithms are at the mercy of the designers and the owners of the platforms, and as we have seen with the recent controversies surrounding Facebook, this alone weakens confidence in them.

Envisaging the next logical step would be — what if you could remove Uber the corporation from Uber the app, or Airbnb the corporation from Airbnb the app? What if the crowd could run the app themselves for the crowd with the same trust?

Enter blockchains, crypto currencies and consequently crypto economics. While the blockchain does not create trust inherently, several nodes of the blockchain network independently validating all transactions for some incentive build that trust. If the Blockchain app did not have enough independent miners, Bitcoin transactions would not have been so trustworthy.

> Crypto economic approaches combine cryptography and economics to create robust decentralised P2P networks that thrive over time despite adversaries attempting to disrupt the network. The cryptography underlying these systems is what makes the P2P communication within the networks secure, and the economics is what incentivises all actors to contribute to the network so that it thrives over time.

The Bitcoin blockchain embodied the trust needed for strangers to exchange money across nations without a second thought. It captured the imagination and billions of dollars in value only after it garnered absolute faith in the underlying technology. Dante Disparte in "Why Blockchain Why Now":

> Blockchains record trust like an atomic clock records time. Unlike trust, time marches ever forward and is irreversible. What if trust could be recorded in the same manner, with exactly the same accuracy and fidelity?
> It is worth noting that bitcoin and the rise of crypto currencies as a trillion-dollar asset class in 2017, was spurred without the oversight of a central bank or monetary authority guaranteeing trust or market conduct. Code and the bitcoin blockchain achieved a level of trust that millions of people,

thousands of regulators and hundreds of enforcement agencies around the world struggle to maintain — all in a fraction of the time, with a higher degree of security and an infinitesimally lower cost.

Truth isn't the same as Blockchain Integrity

It is often implied that anything on the blockchain means truth since the blockchain has absolute integrity and can't be altered. But that's a misconception. The Bitcoin blockchain only achieves truth (transactions validity) in transactions with the help of hundreds of thousands of mining nodes. Miners are incentivised by bitcoins to perform the mining exercise. But there are lots of different blockchains out there, some more robust than others. It is essential to pose relevant questions first before reaching a conclusion on its truthiness index.

For example, are all transactions on the blockchain in the public domain? A bank blockchain may not be willing to expose their transactions to the public at all. Is the consensus algorithm that posts transactions decentralised enough? Governments or regulators operating a blockchain may not allow this in principle. Can the miners validating the transactions understand their essence? In a supply-chain finance blockchain, the miners may not differentiate between fake invoices or multiple bill discounting. Hence, the blockchain is not a magic wand that generates immutable truth. It's just a means to an end in recording the truthiness of our world.

More importantly, a blockchain that has integrity today could lose it in the future. Bitcoin's proof-of-work based systems are designed on the assumption that no single entity controls over 50% of the processing power. But the network of nodes that collectively manage a blockchain evolve with time, and such vital assumptions underpinning the system's integrity may no longer hold. If blockchain technologies are used for applications such as recording title deeds or accounting in companies, it implies maintaining integrity over years and decades, and the mechanisms that ensure the blockchain's integrity need to remain robust over those timescales.

Truthiness by
Stephen Colbert, host of *The Colbert Report*

Though the blockchain is often called a "trustless" ledger, the word is a misnomer. If a trustless system were to be defined as one that has no requirements for authentication and authorisation, then certainly crypto currencies are an example of a trustless system, and blockchains support trustless systems. But as rightly pointed out by Preethi Kasireddy (Medium, Feb 3, 2018):

> Blockchains don't actually eliminate trust. What they do is minimise the amount of trust required from any single actor in the system. They do this by distributing trust among different actors in the system via an economic game that incentivises actors to cooperate with the rules defined by the protocol ... When you digitally transfer value from one account to another on the blockchain, you're trusting the underlying blockchain system to both enable that transfer and ensure sender authenticity and currency validity ... Blockchains have a shared ledger that gives us the absolute truth of the state of the system. It uses mathematics, economics, and game theory to incentivise all parties in the system to reach a "consensus", or coming to an agreement on a single state of this ledger.

Trust in Blockchain Governance

But there is another type of trust, equally important, being reposed in the blockchain which needs sustenance, which Kasireddy calls *Social Consensus (Governance)*:

> Of course, even if the machine consensus works perfectly, we can never guarantee a 100% probability of reaching consensus on other important aspects required to maintain trust in the network. For example, when the underlying network needs to be upgraded, improved, or repaired, we need some way to trust that the network and all its constituents can appropriately handle the changes. In such cases, it's very much a coordination effort amongst constituents, or what I would call a "social consensus" (e.g. governance).
>
> For example, if the blockchain requires an improvement (e.g. better transaction logs), we need a governance mechanism that coordinates the interests of all parties involved (users, developers, investors, etc.) in coming up with the best solution. Or if there's a controversy on the best path forward (e.g. a contentious fork), then a community needs to form a consensus on what to do next. If an agreement can't be reached, the network forks, and people are forced to choose one side over another instead of everyone believing in a shared truth. Users would lose trust in the system because they would be unable to reasonably determine which chain was the "valid" chain.
>
> ...
>
> Perhaps a more accurate way to describe blockchains is not as "trustless," but as built on the basis of distributed trust: We are trusting everyone in aggregate.

Trust the Oracle for the Truth

A different set of trust issues arise when blockchains are used to record real-world asset transactions as against digital asset transactions. It is commonly known as the "Oracle" problem — how to link the digital world with the physical world. For example, if a blockchain records title records of houses, and a ledger entry is to be recorded in the blockchain when the title of a particular house is transferred from A to B, how does the blockchain know if the house has been physically transferred from A to B in the real world. So you need a trusted authority in the physical world to certify that the transaction being recorded on the blockchain has also been executed in reality by handing over possession of the house from A to B. Such a certifying authority or Oracle is the missing link not just for title transfers, but for a host of use-cases like handling products, commodities, art objects, etcetera.

An Oracle can also turn out to be the weakest link because all external data must be vetted by the it. Further, it has to be both centralised and trustworthy, exactly the opposite of what the blockchain proposes to achieve.

The above argument has sometimes been critiqued on the ground that it is not new — it is an old problem of garbage-in-garbage-out (GIGO) inherent to all computer systems. So at best we can say that the blockchain cannot resolve the GIGO problem on its own through its consensus-based trust mechanism.

Hence, just as we saw in the previous chapter that decentralisation is not a binary problem, and that there is no perfectly decentralised model of the blockchain yet, trust and truth are also not binary problems that can be solved easily, and whether for reasons of governance or data vetting, a modicum of trust remains vested with centralised authorities even in a blockchain application.

Cracking Fort Knox

Chinks in a Blockchain's Armour

Trust, but verify.
— Russian proverb

In order to have a decentralised database, you need to have security. In order to have security, you need to have incentives.
— Vitalik Buterin

It is a truism that it is easier to destroy than it is to build. In the physical world, an act of destruction committed by bad actors (terrorists, rogue governments, fraudsters, saboteurs and criminals) undoes what may have taken decades or centuries to build and preserve. There cannot be a more prominent recent example of such destruction than the 9/11 attacks in the United States, in which the twin towers of the World Trade Centre complex were brought down using hijacked airliners by the al-Qaeda. In contrast, their fellow ideologues the Taliban in Afghanistan rained destruction on the Buddhas of Bamiyan, monumental statues of Buddha over 50 metres high, dating back to the 4th and 5th century carved into the cliff-side. Or the sheer scale of instant destruction when two centuries-old cities stood flattened as the first atomic bombs fell on Hiroshima and Nagasaki. It takes little to destroy a lot.

Cyber security faces similar challenges, where malicious programs, viruses and brute-force attacks bring large networks to their knees. Recent infamous examples include *WannaCry* and *NotPetya*, both ransomware. From two *Wired* articles:

> In 2017, security researchers sounded the alarm about Russian hackers infiltrating and probing the United States power companies; there was even evidence that the actors had direct access to an American utility's control systems. Combined with other high-profile Russian hacking from 2017, like the NotPetya ransomware attacks, the grid penetrations were a sobering revelation. It wasn't until this year, though, that the US government began publicly acknowledging the Russian state's involvement in these actions.
>
> The WannaCry ransomware attack has quickly become the worst digital disaster to strike the internet in years, crippling transportation and hospitals globally ... WannaCry has spread with a speed and scale that ransomware has never achieved before. Its use of a recently leaked NSA Windows vulnerability, called EternalBlue, created the worst epidemic of malicious encryption yet seen.

Traditional cyber security builds a "firewall" approach — centralise the data on a server or group of servers and then ring-fence it with layers of programs to control and authenticate access through the network. It also means physically ring-fencing data centres to prevent physical intrusion. The firewall determines which data goes in and which flows out to whom. Breach the firewall with brute-force attacks or some security hole in the code itself, and you gain control of the data. It's a cat-and-mouse game that never ends, and frequent security updates is a pain familiar to even the average cell phone user to guard personal data from theft.

Blockchain security is an antithesis to the "firewall" model since it is a system that is harder to destroy than it is to build. Bitcoin's protocol is public and freely accessible to anyone trying to break it. No one has. Since everyone has a full copy of the ledger, if an attacker could penetrate the cryptographic layer of bitcoin, the system would crumble, but even with immense computing power that would take trillions of years. Bitcoin is impervious to social engineering attacks as well since no one person or group can change it.

There are different broad possibilities by which blockchain-based systems may be compromised in the future.

Cryptography Hacks

While the cryptographic layer may appear impregnable today, future developments in areas like quantum computing may alter the landscape. History testifies that cryptographic schemes can and will be broken; hence crypto tokens will also need to evolve.

Consensus Attacks

The 51% attack has long been discussed as a potential attack vector in Bitcoin. If 51% or more of the hashing power is controlled by one party, that party could prevent transactions from being confirmed and reverse transactions sent. In proof-of-work blockchains like Bitcoin, the cost of mining infrastructure including specialised hardware like ASICs (Application Specific Integrated Circuits) restricts the opportunity of mining to players with deep pockets and in effect reduce decentralisation lowering the security profile of the blockchain system. Similarly, mining pools, where users mine for a pool instead of themselves for a proportionate payout, give the pools more weightage in the network, and over time, a few pools dominate the network, as is currently evident. There are numerous news reports which now state that the Bitcoin mining pools controlled by China-based industry giant Bitmain control over 40% of the total Bitcoin hashrate, and are rapidly moving towards the 51% mark. In 2014, GHash had also briefly gained control of 51% of the network hashrate.

Proof-of-stake systems as employed in the Ethereum blockchain solve the mining centralisation problem by asking miners to put in a financial "stake", instead of computing power. It eliminates the need for expensive hardware as well but comes with its strings attached, such as cartel formation. The latter system remains unproven at scale as well.

All said and done, there are at least a couple of things that even a consensus attack cannot alter. It cannot take away any coins you already possess. And it cannot alter the protocol itself, at least, not without a hard fork.

Long Range or History Revision Attacks

Applicable to blockchains which employ the Proof-of-Stake consensus protocol, a Long Range attack happens when an adversary creates a branch (soft fork) on the blockchain starting from the genesis block longer than the main chain itself with a different set of transactions. In Proof-of-work blockchains like Bitcoin, the longest chain rule is the way to identify the main chain because it is also the one where the maximum physical resources have been expended through mining, and unless a 51% attack is underway, it is not possible to have competing branches because it would need still more computational power. But Proof-of-Stake blockchains use validators and not miners, and computational power is not a factor at all. Hence, in addition to the longest chain rule, a combination of other techniques have to be used in conjunction to mitigate such risks. These include the use of Moving Checkpoints, Context-

Aware Transactions, Key-Evolving Cryptography and the Plenitude Rule, a discussion of all of which is beyond the scope of our text. Suffice to say that none of these offers fool-proof protection as yet.

Social Engineering Attacks

These occur when a person or group of people sabotage a system via psychological manipulation rather than software engineering whether intentionally or unintentionally. Bitcoin, being most decentralised, is most durable to social engineering attacks.

What often builds the perception of fraud in blockchain-based systems is the breach of individual security, such as the loss of private keys. Numerous reports of bitcoins being stolen have all been because of poor security on behalf of individuals, not the systems themselves. The breaches arise because the blockchain has no concept of individual identity, giving a false sense of security to people. Common security operations of authentication and authorisation require use of non-blockchain technologies and all the challenges that come with those technologies.

Crypto currencies use digital signatures to verify that the participants in a transaction are indeed the owners of the currency in the transaction. However, there is no single canonical right way to do digital signatures, and existing approaches are fraught with problems, such as relying on third-party organisations to vet owner identities. Web trackers and cookies can always leak information on the web.

Privacy solutions to prevent breach of individual security are also attracting a great deal of developmental attention, and while explaining them in detail here is beyond the scope at the moment, some areas include using Elliptic Curve Diffie-Hellman-Merkle (ECDHM) addresses, using "mixers" that mix transactions within a group of people or a pool, using alternative protocols like Cryptonote (by the altcoin Monero) which offers a group signature scheme, and Zero-knowledge proofs where a prover convinces a verifier that they have some secret knowledge without revealing the knowledge directly.

Smart Contract Verification

An area of security concern is the verification of smart contracts, that is, a methodology to determine whether the smart contract behaves as per specification. Since smart contracts are immutable and cannot be updated or fixed once deployed on the Ethereum network, we need to ensure they are bug-free to use these contracts in real-world applications. In practice, this is extremely difficult at present.

Unwanted Content Insertion

A widely reported news story deals with a very different ramification of the blockchain. German researchers from the RWTH Aachen University discovered that Bitcoin's distributed ledger is being used to store, besides the regular monetary information, many links and data connected to some hundreds of files with illegal child pornographic content. In their paper titled *Thwarting Unwanted Blockchain Content Insertion*, they state:

> A recent study reveals that over 1600 such files have been irrevocably engraved into Bitcoin's blockchain to be shared in a censorship-resistant manner. These files range from simple text to over 155 images, source codes and PDF files. Any objectionable content, e.g., illegal pornography, in such files is then inevitably distributed to all nodes of the crypto currency's underlying peer-to-peer network. It is expected that court rulings in major jurisdictions such as Germany and

the USA will then find node operators culpable of possessing objectionable content. As a consequence, the node operators must delete affected parts of the blockchain, thereby breaking the blockchain's integrity and verifiability. The insertion of objectionable content has thus the potential of jeopardising crypto currencies as all users ultimately depend on this verification. Indeed, recent research finds that, while most content is likely harmless, Bitcoin's blockchain already today contains content that is objectionable in many jurisdictions, e.g., an image of a nude young woman or hundreds of links to child pornography.

Buterin himself highlights how the Blockchain, with all its attendant benefits of decentralisation, cannot be immune to failure and its fault-tolerance, attack-resistance and collusion-resistance can all be compromised (*The Meaning of Decentralisation,* Medium Feb 6, 2017):

> Consider the following scenarios:
> All nodes in a blockchain run the same client software, and this client software turns out to have a bug.
> All nodes in a blockchain run the same client software, and the development team of this software turns out to be socially corrupted.
> The research team that is proposing protocol upgrades turns out to be socially corrupted.
> In a proof-of-work blockchain, 70% of miners are in the same country, and the government of this country decides to seize all mining farms for national security purposes.
> The majority of mining hardware is built by the same company, and this company gets bribed or coerced into implementing a back-door that allows this hardware to be shut down at will.
> In a proof-of-stake blockchain, 70% of the coins at stake are held at one exchange.

Collusion Resistance

From an attack-resistance perspective for blockchains, Buterin favours proof-of-stake over proof-of-work as computer hardware is easy to detect, regulate and attack, whereas coins can be much more easily hidden. He favours having widely distributed development teams, including geographic distribution. But on collusion resistance, Buterin says:

> In the case of blockchain protocols, the mathematical and economic reasoning behind the safety of the consensus often relies crucially on the uncoordinated choice model, or the assumption that the game consists of many small actors that make decisions independently. If any one actor gets more than 1/3 of the mining power in a proof-of-work system, they can gain outsized profits by selfish-mining. However, can we really say that the uncoordinated choice model is realistic when 90% of the Bitcoin network's mining power is well-coordinated enough to show up together at the same conference?
>
> Blockchain advocates also make the point that blockchains are more secure to build on because they can't just change their rules arbitrarily on a whim whenever they want to, but this case would be difficult to defend if the developers of the software and protocol were all working for one company, were part of one family and sat in one room. The whole point is that these systems should not act like self-interested unitary monopolies. Hence, you can certainly make a case that blockchains would be more secure if they were more discoordinated.

Cryptojacking

The saga of the Monero coin (XMR), which ranked in the top ten crypto currencies, is just a reminder that such security vulnerabilities have already been exploited in the past, and the cycle continues. Secret ASICs had been developed to mine Monero since early 2017 and were discovered only in 2018 when Monero hard-forked to shake them off, and it is estimated that in that period these secret ASICs controlled over 50% of the hashrate rendering Monero vulnerable to a 51% attack. Similarly, many other coins are also the target of such ASIC mining attempts by an underground mining industry. But escaping from the clutches of ASIC Miners by hard-forking, Monero has plunged into a different kind of problem — that of surreptitious use of computers and phones worldwide to mine it. Hackers have commandeered huge processing power to mine Monero using malware to run calculations. The malware was found on over 4,000 sites, including those owned by the governments of U.S., Australia and Britain.

Cryptojacking, the new term being used to describe this phenomenon, is the unauthorised use of someone else's computer to mine crypto currency, and represents one more in the list of security hazards, albeit on the user side of the blockchain.

Governmental Interference

Governments around the world and throughout history have not shied away from a subversive action whenever someone or something — even a technology — has threatened their power and control apparatus. Wikileaks 2010 release of the US State Department memos followed by the Edward Snowden's breach of US Intelligence systems and leaks in 2013 brought home these issues with a bang.

Here are a couple of seemingly outrageous scenarios that impact blockchain security which, while improbable, are not impossible. What if a government monopolised mining by investing in an ASIC data-centre so huge that other miners failed? Or what if it launched a covert operation to simply eliminate all developers behind a particular blockchain?

The truth is that at least in the case of Bitcoin the governments have a much easier option. Just turn off the electricity. The fact that the Bitcoin blockchain guzzles electricity through its mining operations — something we discuss in detail as part of its scalability problem in the next chapter — makes it vulnerable since electricity is a commodity directly or indirectly under the control of governments. In January 2018, China's central bank did order curbs on mining activity by limiting access to power. Canada's Hydro-Quebec adopted a pick-and-choose policy for miners to whom they want to supply with electricity. The giant mining farms are at the mercy of a switch. Another way to look at this vulnerability is through land use. Ultimately miners have to be geographically located somewhere, and that again implies sovereign control.

For a young technology, the blockchain has to surmount considerable challenges on the security front. The trust in a blockchain's immutability forms the bedrock of its token's (currency's) value and is a direct function of its security. As is the scalability of the blockchain itself. All of which leads to an interesting dilemma, or rather trilemma, the subject of our next chapter.

The Scalability Trilemma

To Grow, or Not to Grow

Today's mighty oak is just yesterday's nut, that held its ground.
— David Icke

The Scalability Trilemma says that a blockchain can only have two of the following three properties: decentralisation, scalability (or speed), and security.

That is, given a level of security, to increase a blockchain's scalability (or speed), its decentralisation must be sacrificed. Why is this true?

Since every single validating node needs to run every single computation that occurs on the network to ensure its accuracy, for a network having thousands of nodes running validators to be sufficiently decentralised, the maximum number of transactions per second will be capped by what the average node's computer and network speed can handle.

Blockchains today can only process a limited number of transactions — Bitcoin processes a block every 10 minutes while Ethereum does it every 14 seconds (most bloggers and authors benchmark this speed with that of Visa or Mastercard networks to highlight the contrast, which process approximately 2000 transactions per second versus 5 to 7 for Bitcoin and 100 for Ethereum). On the other hand, scaling the blockchain and speeding up transactions would require that all nodes be super-computers and have as few nodes as possible on the network to decrease the number of connections per node. Putting all the nodes in the same geographical area or data-centre would further decrease latency. But all these measures would drastically reduce decentralisation.

Solutions to the Trilemma

A lot of energy in the blockchain ecosystem is currently focussed on finding solutions around this scalability trilemma.

A very logical one is to reduce the number of transactions that need to be captured by the blockchain by storing them in conventional database structures and use the blockchain as a settlement or summary layer and capture only the final transaction in a given series. The conventional databases meet the speed and scalability requirements for individual transactions while the blockchain meets the immutability and "truth" requirements at the summary level. An example of this model is the micro-payment processor Lightning Network (https://lightning.network).

Sharding

Another solution derives inspiration from a load-sharing technology for conventional database systems called Sharding. It is a type of "horizontal partitioning" of the database where each partition is called a "shard" and held on a separate database server instance.

When applied to blockchains, sharding implies that each node in the blockchain network only contains a part of the ledger or a shard, a concept in many ways antithetical to its founding principles. Numerous nodes will maintain a single shard achieving decentralisation within while promoting overall scalability that is obtained by not loading the entire ledger on every node. But it also implies that in such a scenario of partial information a consensus algorithm like proof-of-work will not work. Hence newer consensus algorithms like proof-of-stake (PoS) are used.

Under PoS, only designated mining nodes called "stakers" validate the transaction and not the entire network. It eliminates the need for mining, saving energy. Stakers deposit crypto tokens as a stake before validation, and upon successful validation, earn a part or whole of the transaction fee. More the crypto tokens that are staked, and the longer the duration of the stake, the higher the number of transactions that the node validates building higher loyalty, which is the key to ensuring that the security of the blockchain is not compromised. The whole idea of the stake is as insurance against foul play. In case the stakers tamper with the blockchain, their stake stands forfeited. An example of this model is the Shard Coin (SHARD).

Sharding can not only improve the speed at which transactions are processed but also solve the storage problem simultaneously. Since in a normal blockchain, each node carries the full ledger which is not only immutable but of an ever-increasing size into the future, data storage will also impose a considerable cost. Sharding eases out this problem up-front by splitting storage in shards distributed over the participating nodes. Some projects mentioned earlier in the context of dApps — IPFS and StorJ — allow files to be stored and retrieved in a decentralised fashion using such ideas.

Ethereum's roadmap and Buterin's recent announcements indicate that Ethereum is ready to roll out together two of its most anticipated updates — Sharding and Casper. Casper is Ethereum's PoS consensus algorithm and might be released on a shard, rather than as a smart contract. With another project underway called Plasma, Buterin has claimed that with all these solutions put in place, the Ethereum network will eventually be able to process one million transactions per second and potentially scale up to more than a hundred million transactions per second. Plasma is a technique for conducting off-chain transactions while relying on the underlying Ethereum blockchain to ground its security, similar to the Bitcoin's Lightning Network mentioned earlier.

Sidechains

A recent development that can help enhance the capabilities of existing blockchains are the "Sidechains". A Sidechain is a separate blockchain that is attached to its parent blockchain, with a two-way communication protocol that allows exchanging tokens and digital assets between the two.

Each sidechain is independent and must be backed by sufficient mining power of its own for its operations and security. In case a sidechain is hacked, the damage will be restricted to within the chain without affecting the parent blockchain. Sidechains are thus useful for experimenting with beta releases of altcoins before pushing them onto the main chain. Plasma, mentioned briefly in the last paragraph, takes this idea even further by allowing child-chains to spawn their child-chains, which can themselves have another set of child-chains etcetera. So Plasma is effectively many branching blockchains linked to one root blockchain.

There are other things that impact blockchain scalability as well. In Ethereum and its smart contracts, there is the Oracle problem we discussed previously that crops up when we link the digital world with the physical world. The Oracle can also turn out to be the weakest link in the chain demanding both centralisation and trust.

Fragmentation Limits Growth

Fragmentation in the blockchain space with many different blockchains, each having its protocol, automatically limits their growth prospects. The technology industry has repeatedly demonstrated that more than the superior platform, it is the one which acquires a critical mass of users and developers first that wins the race. Bitcoin had a first-mover advantage, and Ethereum had radical innovation over Bitcoin as a second-generation platform with enhanced capabilities, and hence both met with considerable success.

But with so many blockchains being launched subsequently, most of which are just variations on a theme, gaining a growing base of users becomes a great challenge, and they cannot scale to size. So of the Multichain (s), R3-Corda (s), Hyperledger (s), EOS (s), Waves and so many others of the blockchain world, few will pass muster in time. Consolidation in the industry is a must for its scalability.

Energy — Bitcoin is not Green

Finally, an area of concern that limits scalability, at least in case of the Bitcoin blockchain, and not mentioned as part of the trilemma, is energy. Bitcoin miners spend massive amounts of computing power to run the computations that solve the proof-of-work algorithm, but unfortunately, all of this computational work has no value to society. Bitcoin's estimated annual electricity consumption stands at over 30TWh, which is more electricity than 159 individual countries. And a lot of this energy may not be coming from sustainable sources. A meme puts it across that this is just China exporting coal over the internet — China burns coal and pollutes their air to mine bitcoins which they sell to the West who then "Hodl" them. Hence, while the beauty of the Bitcoin consensus mechanism is that it is open and permissionless, its flip side is that it is not green and sustainable, thus hampering scalability.

However, with other blockchain platforms adopting different proofs-of-validity which are much more energy-efficient in arriving at a consensus to validate transactions, this may not pose much of a barrier to them.

The trade-offs discussed above make solving the trilemma a work of art, where achieving the right balance of relying on some form of central authority with a precise transaction-processing speed in a reasonably secure environment will present a continuous challenge. Each network will hold out its promise — a Bitcoin-like network where the currency application is paramount may focus on the highest levels of security that cannot be manipulated or attacked even by governments, versus an Ethereum-like network where the platform rules would carry much more sanctity so that developers of dApps do not fear arbitrary changes. But of course, the perfect combination will never be achieved.

Like perfect markets and perpetual machines, the fully secure, blazingly-fast decentralised blockchain with an infinite storage space can only be an ideal assumption, not reality.

Part III

Maslow's Hammer

(Mis)Use Cases

> I suppose it is tempting, if the only tool you have is a hammer, to treat everything as if it were a nail.
> — Abraham Maslow in 1966 (*Wikipedia*)

Technologies which appear to shift the paradigm stimulate the quirks in human psychology. There is always a palpable sense of excitement and anticipation of the next big thing. Even with the knowledge that things are but cyclical, especially in technology, where many such anticipated shifts have proven to be straws in the wind, there emerges the steadfast belief that "this time is different" (because technologists suffer identical delusions as stock-pickers). People forget or ignore the lessons of the most recent cycle, like the dot com boom and bust, and rush in with money, wanting in at any cost, and the blockchain is no exception to this euphoria. Every database application is but a nail for the blockchain hammer because blockchain is the best. Well, not really.

Blockchains cannot supplant conventional databases. They have certain admirable features, discussed extensively in this book so far, which makes blockchains an ideal fit for applications like crypto currencies where conventional databases would never have succeeded, and bitcoin is a testimony to that. That blockchains can host and enable decentralised applications and help build open tokenised networks is by itself pretty promising. But almost 99% of our existing digital applications are better off design-wise in their current state and gain next to nothing if they switch their architecture to the blockchain.

Let us look briefly at the deterrents and then at specific use-cases.

First, almost all existing applications (or ledgers) are centralised in control. Replacing a conventional database at the back-end with a blockchain does not alter the centralised control, rather it replaces a fast and efficient database with a slow and inefficient one.

Second, we have already seen that storage costs in a blockchain are really high, because every node stores the full ledger. While the use of sharding in blockchains may ease this problem going forward, it is no match for the storage efficiency of the conventional databases.

Third, the transaction processing speed of blockchains makes them appear as slow lumbering giants, and thus unsuited to the super-fast transaction processing needs of many of the existing applications.

Fourth, scaling a blockchain is only possible by reducing the number and increasing the power of the individual nodes — which is nothing but centralisation in the first place. So why bother?

And last but not the least, blockchain development and execution is costly.

Smartness in Smart Contracts

Nomenclature can be somewhat deceptive, for "smartness" implies utopian qualities in contracts built on some AI-like magic. In reality things are mundane. A smart contract is just a regular program which reads and writes data from and to the blockchain's (distributed) database. The code of the program also lives within the same database so it may be looked upon as the equivalent of a "stored procedure" in conventional databases. Blockchain transactions can trigger its execution thus altering the blockchain's state. The only additional characteristic is that when triggered, the code must run independently on every node and arrive at a consensus result before it alters the blockchain's state.

If such a smart contract or program is to respond to external events, the same information must be fetched by every node on the chain, and there must be a guarantee that this information will not alter in the meantime, or the blockchain consensus will fail.

That will lead us back to the need for a centralised "Oracle" that will guarantee this. Having a trusted entity to manage the interactions between the blockchain and the outside world undermines the goal of a decentralised system, and it's simpler to have a conventional database at the backend rather than a blockchain.

An oft-cited example of smart contracts is their potential use to automate payment of interest on bonds and loans, along with the principal when due. But to guarantee such timely payments, the funds must be at the exclusive disposal of the smart contract, which would preclude their use anywhere else. In case the funds are at the disposal of any other entity in the system, which they will be because that is decidedly the idea behind any bond issuance or loan appraisal, then the blockchain smart contract cannot guarantee timely payment. It would result in a stalemate, because a blockchain smart contract cannot transform what is by definition a risky bond, howsoever low risk, into a risk-free one by guaranteeing all the payouts over time.

Permissioned and Private Blockchains

As opposed to the "open" blockchain defined at the beginning of our chapter "Blockchain 101" — decentralised, public and peer-to-peer like Bitcoin and Ethereum — it is equally possible to build a blockchain closed in some respects. It may mean that its ledger is not accessible publicly, or that everyone is not free to join the network without permission from those governing the blockchain. Or maybe the mining nodes are closely controlled for authenticating transactions, or dispensed with altogether if the blockchain designers do not use proof-of-work for authentication, which then reduces the status of the blockchain to just a shared ledger. Depending on the spectrum of constraints, such a blockchain may be called a Permissioned Blockchain or a Private one.

Use cases for such blockchains exist in inter-bank clearing and money-transfer applications, private logistics networks and other areas. While the wisdom of banks and fintech companies adopting permissioned blockchains is debated below, the point to note here is that if banks are fixated on the idea, they have no choice but to adopt these constraints. No bank would ever be willing to share its ledger publicly revealing confidential client information. Neither would any bank be willing to broadcast a transaction publicly just for the sake of authentication from miners. They would want miners within their networks whom they can control. There may be cooperation between banks for clearing and money transfer purposes or to share credit ratings of clients, and such a shared network built on permissioned blockchain technology can help conserve overall computing resources and improve security at the cost of sacrificing network speed, the inevitable trade-off.

Nevertheless, one of the chief features of the blockchain — decentralisation — is lost wholly in such use-cases, and the same result is perfectly achievable with the existing database systems as well. Ripple, one of the most cited and successful examples, is analysed later in this chapter.

Purists, however, stand by their point of view that a centralised, permissioned or private blockchain is an oxymoron.

Media of late has been chock-a-block with announcements and the launch of blockchain projects across the spectrum. Discussed here are some such projects and announcements where, to a discerning analyst, there is no use-case for the blockchain at all, yet Maslow's hammer is hitting each one serially. Let us begin with the banks.

Banks and Fintech on the Blockchain

The biggest-ticket announcements have stemmed from the banks and the fintech sector where consortiums have been established to build different versions of blockchains and apps — by "market disruptors" like R3 and Digital Asset Holdings LLC.

In 2017, Bank of America Merill Lynch, Wells Fargo, HSBC, Deutsche Bank, HSBC, Reuters and even Intel invested $107 million in R3 product "Corda" blockchain. R3 also announced the integration of their blockchain product with SAP in the case of Commerzbank. R3 then announced another trade finance network "Marco Polo" based on the same Corda blockchain technology but this time including BNP Paribas, ING, Commerzbank, Standard Chartered, DNB and others. Digital Asset, a competitor to R3 raised a $110 million of its own from private investors, and had formed its consortiums including Goldman Sachs and JP Morgan. The latter is also a member of the blockchain consortium Enterprise Ethereum Alliance as well as the Hyperledger Project of the Linux Foundation. The Wall Street Journal list of top technology companies, dominated by blockchain companies, profiled both R3 and Digital Asset on that list.

Banks claim they are funding and building these private blockchain networks to settle their transactions more efficiently. Blockchain certainly helps in creating a shared ledger among banks to settle their swaps or other financial product transactions and save "billions of dollars". But it's interesting to analyse why banks spend billions of dollars in these transaction settlements in the first place. It's primarily due to legacy mainframe systems in the banks' back offices and workflows that are decades old, need high maintenance to keep running and are coupled with inefficient manual processes on top. Banks can achieve similar savings if they replace their back-office systems with any efficient shared database technologies like Oracle, SQL and layer some smart business logic on top of them. Besides, banks' blockchain networks are private among those that know each other and have several legal contracts between them and do not need or intend to use any independent mining. Hence, blockchain serves minimal purpose in these scenarios, if any.

Similar is the case of fintech and payment processors. You would be hard-pressed to find one that announced a blockchain use-case or proof-of-concept years ago and then actually issued a successful "scaled-up blockchain transactions" press release after the initial announcement. Here is an extract from an article in *Forbes* by Jeff John Roberts, July 17, 2018:

> In 2015, digital payments giant Stripe unveiled a tool for merchants around the world to accept Bitcoin. At the time, Stripe's news came as further evidence that a crypto currency revolution was underway. But this April, Stripe pulled the plug.
> What happened? According to Stripe COO Claire Hughes Johnson, speaking at Fortune's Brainstorm Tech conference on Tuesday, Bitcoin and other blockchain-based payment services are slow, impractical, and over-hyped.
> She noted that clearance times for a Bitcoin transaction right

now are about 60 minutes, and that last December it reached three to five days. Hughes Johnson said the backlog was so bad that merchants sometimes had to file a second transaction to account for bitcoin price fluctuations that occurred between when a purchase occurred and when it cleared.

So should it have surprised anyone when R3 too made its announcement abandoning blockchain technology altogether after spending US$59 million on its research? Corda would no longer be based on the blockchain technology, and R3's altered its description from that of a "blockchain startup" to a "blockchain inspired startup". The irony, though, seems to be lost on the banks themselves, who continue to pour in funds at record speed.

Real Estate on the Blockchain

Real estate has been traditionally driven by paper-based title records and involves a lot of third-party players, including brokers and banks. A blockchain-based design would definitely allow people to transfer funds, property titles and data in a peer-to-peer manner that is digital and open source. Dubai Land Department announced the creation of a blockchain-based system using a smart and secure database to record all real estate contracts, including lease registrations, linking the dealer, land apartment management companies, phone and internet service providers, furnishing solution providers and even the banks. All this would be done by linking the user's blockchain profile to his Dubai ID and would contain all remaining information. Similarly, Deloitte announced the development of a platform to handle rental and other real estate contracts digitally and invited Commercial Real Estate (CRE) companies and industry participants evaluating an upgrade or overhaul of their current systems to have blockchain on their radar. A third service provider, Ubitquity, announced a blockchain-secured platform for real estate transactions offering a simple user experience for securely recording, tracking, and transferring deeds. The platform prototype was released in March 2016 as a Software-as-a-Service (SaaS) blockchain platform. Ubitquity also claimed to provide e-recording companies, title companies, municipalities and custom clients benefits from a clean record of ownership, thereby reducing future title search time, and increasing confidence/transparency. Citing a Lands Record Bureau in Brazil as one of their early clients, they claim to "use multiple permissioned and permissionless blockchains in an effort to remain fully blockchain-agnostic".

The problems in this use-case stem from the indispensability of paperwork, issues over transparency and time taken to execute transfers. Given that property deals are always going to be approved by some central authority or the other like a Municipal corporation, or an appointed Government body, the decision-making aspect of property transactions shall always be centralised. In such cases, using a technology which touts decentralisation as its chief purpose is antithetical and purposeless. As far as the problem of digitisation of the paperwork and bringing transparency in the transactions process is concerned, this could be easily achieved by digitising land records, and making the transfer process online where the buyers/sellers can raise their request online and approving agencies can approve it online too. It does not need a blockchain at all. Ubitquity is building on some shaky stilts.

Diamonds on the Blockchain

In the 1971 film, *Diamonds Are Forever*, Bond's nemesis Blofeld and his secretive SPECTRE organisation use diamond smuggling to fund a space-based laser weapon. In Bond's 2002 film *Die Another Day*, his adversary ran an empire on conflict diamonds a.k.a. blood diamonds, something that also fuelled Sierra Leone's long civil war and insurgency. And there is no heist that excites gangsters more than a diamond heist. So it makes a lot of sense to record a gem on a blockchain documenting its provenance and future sales.

Everledger, a startup, claimed to have proven this possibility by logging the identifying characteristics of over 1.6 million diamonds on the blockchain, information that would be useful to various stakeholders — from claimants to insurance companies to law enforcement agencies, making counterfeit claims impossible.

Little wonder then that IBM also announced TrustChain on its blockchain platform in collaboration with Asahi Refining, Helzberg Diamonds, LeachGarner, Richline Group and Underwriters Labs. Participants in the blockchain network hope to keep track of all components in a piece of jewellery easily from the time they are mined, as they're fabricated into consumer products, such as diamond engagement rings, and until they're sold. Block Verify, another blockchain startup, claims to end counterfeiting and make the world more secure.

The problem in these use cases is the unique identification of assets like diamonds. It is the same problem with paintings (where, for example, an artist draws only five paintings to keep them exclusive and hence priced higher). The challenge arises when people make and sell fake diamonds or fake paintings. What is not being decentralised here is the consensus on what's original and what's fake. That shall always be controlled by the firm producing the diamonds or some other central authority appointed by the diamond firms, or a curator or museum in the case of paintings.

If all that is needed is a unique digital stamp on each diamond, which can then be easily traced and tracked by the issuer firm, and since such digital stamping mechanisms like QR codes, etcetera exist and are readily available, there is no need for the blockchain at all. We have already discussed the "Oracle" problem of blockchains when it comes to physical assets in the chapter The Scalability Trilemma, and since diamonds, paintings and precious jewellery all constitute physical assets, the blockchain cannot track them without a central intermediary to certify that the physical asset in question corresponds to one on the blockchain record. It effectively nullifies any blockchain advantage since that very same central intermediary can in any case directly certify the asset in question to be genuine or fake.

Ripples' Payment Mechanism on the Blockchain

Ripple has emerged as one of the early movers and a formidable player in the domain of real-time gross settlement of funds, currency exchange and remittance. It has in a short span of time built a global network of participating banks and payment providers. The Ripplenet blockchain network, using the token (cryptocurrency) Ripple (XRP) is meant to enable instant and direct transfer of money between two parties, and the exchange of any fiat currency, commodity or asset.

While the general impression is that Ripple is a permissioned blockchain, that is, a blockchain whose mining mechanism to validate transactions is private and controlled, the truth is somewhat different. As succinctly explained by the *Blockchain Magazine*:

> It is the validating servers and consensus mechanism that tends to lead people to assume that Ripple is a blockchain-based technology. While it is consensus-oriented, Ripple is not a blockchain. Ripple uses a HashTree to summarise the data into a single value that is compared across its validating servers to provide consensus.
>
> Banks seem to like Ripple, and payment providers are coming on board more and more. It is built for enterprise and, while it can be used person-to-person, that really isn't its primary

focus. The main purpose of the Ripple platform is to move lots of money around the world as rapidly as possible.

Thus far, Ripple has been stable since its release with over 35 million transactions processed without issue. It is able to handle 1,500 transactions per second (tps) and has been updated to be able to scale to Visa levels of 50,000 transactions per second. By comparison, Bitcoin can handle 3-6 tps (not including scaling layers) and Ethereum 15 tps.

Ripple's token, XRP, isn't mined like Bitcoin, Ethereum, Litecoin and many other crypto currencies. Instead, it was issued at its inception, similar in fashion to the way a company issues stocks when it incorporates: It essentially just picked a number (100 billion) and issued that many XRP coins.

As a technology, the Ripple platform may have real value and real history that validate the claims they make for its efficacy. The XRP token itself, however, seems to have negligible use cases. In fact, Ripple had planned to phase it out — at least, until fevered interest in crypto currencies began to take off in 2016 … The use of XRP is totally independent of the Ripple network in general; that is, banks don't actually need XRP to transfer dollars, euros, etcetera which is what many small investors might be missing when they are buying the token.

Thus, an appropriate way to view Ripple is as a super-efficient SWIFT network rather than as a breakthrough application for the blockchain (SWIFT is the current global payment transfer mechanism used by banks, known to be slow and cumbersome). Often touted as one of the most successful examples of the blockchain implementation, it is anything but, since it is not blockchain-based in the first place.

Travel on the Blockchain

The Amadeus IT Group, owners of Amadeus, the most extensive global distribution system (GDS) for airlines tickets in the worldwide, recently announced their foray into the blockchain space. They stated that it would make travelling easier and streamline the process of making payments, verification of traveller IDs, luggage tracking etc. by reducing the intermediaries and settlement timing while increasing the overall flow transparency. Fast, secure and a simplified ID verification of travellers at every stage seems to be the primary use case for a blockchain.

The fallacy, once again, is that the blockchain is serving no real purpose, because this problem of ID verification at different stages can be solved merely by sharing the access of pre-approved tokens amongst the separate entities constituting the value chain. It is very similar to the way in which you log in to many websites using your Google login which involves no blockchain because there is no decentralisation or consensus involved. If anything, it is the exact opposite.

Supply Chain on the Blockchain

Project Provenance Ltd. has built a blockchain platform Provenance — "A platform that empowers brands to take steps toward greater transparency by tracing the origins and histories of products. With our technology, you can easily gather and verify stories, keep them connected to physical things and embed them anywhere online."

IBM and Walmart have teamed up to launch the Blockchain Food Safety Alliance in China in conjunction with JD.com to improve food tracking and safety, making it easier to verify that food is safe to consume. Proper implementation of the ledger could also prove valuable for pharmaceutical giants, which are required by law to maintain the chain of custody over every pill.

Skuchain and NTT Data announced their partnership in a blockchain supply chain venture.

These use-cases will all suffer identical problems similar to that of tracking diamonds on the blockchain, notably the Oracle problem which occurs when blockchain transactions are linked to physical product movements. In any case, tracking of food or any other products in a supply chain, manufacturing process, or in transit with couriers, Amazon deliveries and Uber car arrivals are all done on simple online platforms using MIS, or any other basic data technologies at the backend. There is no need for any consensus and decentralisation here, and hence, this does not need a blockchain solution at all.

The Walmart announcement follows their previously failed attempt in 2006 to launch a system to track its bananas and mangoes from the field to store, abandoned in 2009 due to logistical problems getting everyone to enter the data in the system. So what failed on account of data entry is highly unlikely to succeed just because you replace the previous database with a blockchain one.

Blockchain or not, any supply chain solution needs to meet two vital prerequisites — everyone's participation in the chain, and honest involvement at that. The garbage-in-garbage-out principle does not exempt the blockchain. In case the data being entered is not clean, the blockchain compounds the problem by making records on it non-editable. Bottom line, it is the human element and compliance that is the more significant challenge in supply chains, not the technology.

Documents on the Blockchain

Bank guarantees are essential in sectors such as real estate, where they represent security for tenants' leases, or where companies need to demonstrate that they can pay for expensive goods. However, bank guarantees can get mislaid, and clients may find the process of handling them to be too laborious and slow. Which is why technology companies are now promising a solution on the blockchain — the Israeli lender Bank Hapoalim and Microsoft announced a collaboration on creating digital bank guarantees based on the blockchain technology. The new process will enable Bank Hapoalim customers to receive security documents in a digital, automated and secure manner, without physically coming to the branch and in a very short process

It is a classic case of finding a complex solution to a simple problem — that of digitising documents and signing them online. Several types of authentication apps for scanning and digital signing exist already. There is absolutely no decentralised consensus needed. A blockchain solution is just overkill.

Shipping and Insurance on the Blockchain

Another announcement in the supply chain space is that EY has teamed up with Maersk and Microsoft on blockchain-based Marine insurance. When shipping goods from port A to port B, any number of things can go wrong: cargo may get damaged, a congested port may delay docking, a storm may throw a vessel off-course or pirates may raid a ship. So shippers buy insurance through a complex jumble of brokers and underwriters to manage the risk to their freight. Ideally, a blockchain should be an absolute fit for this platform, as it will guarantee that all the parties — from the shipping companies to brokers, insurers and the other suppliers — would have access to the same database which could also be integrated into their insurance contracts.

However, in practice, the information flow and approvals are between a few entities only (say the buyer, the seller and two or three banks in the above example). They can achieve the same by digital signatures while sharing the documents through a digital platform (including a simple email server). No independent mining is needed nor can it help in this case; hence a blockchain is undoubtedly not the best solution.

The biggest challenge of a supplier faking invoices, or taking multiple financing from different banks for the same invoice, cannot be solved by the blockchain either, unless all potential financiers become part of the same network, and mine/validate every single transaction; which is asking too much and unlikely to happen in the foreseeable future.

Also, shared databases like SQL and Oracle have existed for decades, and collaboration among different entities in the value chain for validation of such documents has existed for an equally long time. If the validation of any documents and information is to be done by a few entities, access control-based data solutions can do the job just fine. Insurers would want to control this workflow and final approvals anyway. Hence, this does not need blockchain at all.

Governance on the Blockchain

Samsung has won a contract for a public-sector blockchain for South Korea's government to be put to use in public safety and transport applications. However, it is unlikely to achieve its desired goal due to the two perennial bug-bears of all government processes — centralised workflow and decision making. In most scenarios, the functioning of a blockchain is the very antithesis of the working of a government, and mating of these opposites remains a distant dream.

Media on the Blockchain

Kodak recently sent its stock soaring after announcing that it is developing a blockchain system for tracking intellectual property rights and payments to photographers. As one of the oldest names in the imaging business, it is leveraging the blockchain technology to fix problems that have been plaguing the photography industry for a while. Kodak and WENN Digital have joined hands to launch a blockchain-powered image rights management platform, dubbed as KODAKOne, along with a photo-centric crypto currency, to be known as KODAKcoin. Kodak's platform takes the whole photography and imaging industry to a new level with all the features of distributed ledger technology like encryption, decentralisation, immutability, transparency and security being utilised to create a digital ledger of 'ownership rights' for photographers. The digital ledger will secure the work of photographers by registering work and then allowing them to license the same for use (buy/sell) within the platform.

However, the Kodakcoin concept can only work if the community drives the coin and the platform. But that may not help Kodak much as it will just decentralise itself away as a node. Given that Kodak is not likely to let that happen, this use case is only self-serving, and the community will not believe in it. Hence, the blockchain will be infructuous.

In the end, you may be tempted to ask the only logical question — is the blockchain good for nothing then? Not at all.

The incontrovertible and proven blockchain application is, of course, the crypto currency bitcoin. That for the first time in human history we have a currency, a digital one too, which is not a fiat currency, not controlled by any authority, freely transferable at negligible cost as if the world were suddenly rendered borderless, that alone suffices as the blockchain's raison d'être.

Even if the blockchain never throws up another application, which is undoubtedly far from the truth, it would still rank as a breakthrough of stupendous proportions in human economic and technological advancement.

The final chapter of the book is an exploration of how the blockchain is a futuristic technology that will serve as one of the foundational pillars in conjunction with others like Artificial Intelligence, Internet of Things and Quantum Computing.

Meanwhile, we still have some substantial ground to cover before that — a deeper revisit of ICOs and the embedded value in tokens, ICO regulation, and the emerging areas of Reverse ICOs, Crypto ETFs, Crypto Custody and Crypto Insurance.

A Coin for your Thoughts

Valuation and Regulation Conundrums

As long as the music is playing, you've got to get up and dance.
— Chuck Prince, former chairman and chief executive of Citigroup, in the wake of the sub-prime meltdown

The killer app for Bitcoin out there today is ransomware.
— quoted in *Forbes*, July 17, 2018

There's a long list of existential questions that have puzzled humanity through the ages around which the debates still rage. Well, you can add a new one to that list now — what represents the fair value of digital tokens that are born, live and die on the internet? How should they be regulated?

With over twenty billion dollars having already flown into ICOs in less than two years, millions of people now own crypto currencies, and token prices flash, ebb and rise in an unceasing dance on computer screens across the world. Exchanges hum round-the-clock and announcements tweet every second. Yet in this din, there are prominent voices which remain sceptical. What, they ask, is the value of any crypto currency, or crypto token? Speculation aside, what are the factors that determine its fundamental value? Is zero regulation the panacea it is made to be? Reasonable questions from reasonable people, though often dismissed by others by labelling these people as lacking imagination, or guts, or as relics of a bygone era who just don't get it.

At the opposite end of the spectrum, are people who view ICOs through the prism of scams and get-rich schemes. For them, ICOs are just an avenue to speculate by another name. Many institutional investors who adopt this mindset appear to be driven solely by the greater-fool theory — that as long as there is another buyer in the chain, it time to invest. It's a mania, and all manias are the same, from the Dutch tulipomania to the recent US housing bubble. ICOs are nothing but crypto mania that may burst anytime.

The truth, as usual, lies somewhere in the middle. Yes, the internet changed our lives fundamentally. And yes, it underwent a massive bubble of its own, when a dot com having zero business prospects could command some very frosty valuations. The parallels to the crypto space are inescapable. And therefore, the benefits would lie beyond the bubble, which must burst for us to reap them. As in any boom-bust, it is the small guy who must pay the price. Such is the nature of progress and human psychology.

Value in a Digital Token

What's important to understand is that the digital token is a new beast on the block. It will not yield itself to a conventional approach. The new tools — the theoretical infrastructure that will win the Nobels and the university dons who will expound these theories — are still distant. What is amply clear now is that crypto tokens are the drivers of the decentralised networks which connect humans, bots and machines. They are the missing link because of which, even though the internet was always decentralised, the networks were centralised. Suddenly open-source also has a business model — a way to incentivise the creation of new protocols and govern them well.

To understand this a little better, consider that the original internet protocols (such as HTTP and TCP/IP) were open-source and decentralised, yet they only defined how data is delivered and were stateless. However, for any application to function, the data layer was indispensable, which was provided by the companies building the applications themselves, resulting in centralisation. Further, these protocols also did not provide end-to-end security nor any incentives for innovation. All investments focussed on the application layer to make up for these shortcomings.

Tokens, for the first time, managed to fix the incentive problem, providing people with the right impetus to develop the protocols, besides the benefits of decentralisation and security. Historically, the only way to make money from a protocol was to create software that implemented it and then try to sell or host this software, always a tall order. With tokens, however, the creators of a protocol could "monetise" it directly, and then benefit more as others built businesses on top of that protocol.

This concept of how the blockchain adds value is sometimes called the "fat protocol" as illustrated below:

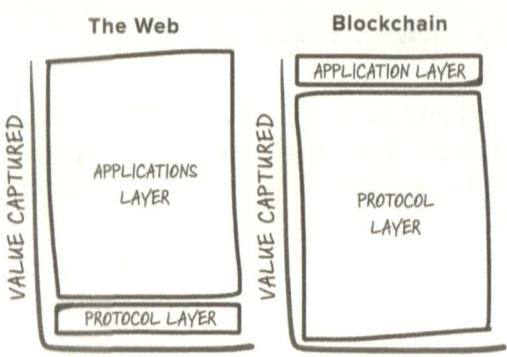

Fat Protocol (Image : USV Website)

From the *Convergence Ecosystem Report* by Outlier Ventures (March 2018) on types of digital tokens and the value they represent:

> Experimentation is happening at a rapid pace on both the supply and demand side. We have tokens with a deflationary economy, scheduled inflation and others that let the community vote on how and when new tokens are minted and/or burned. That is just programmable money supply; we are also experimenting with demand-side economics: variable transaction fees, demurrage charges, interoperability and different consensus rules. Non-fungible tokens such as cryptokitties and the new Ethereum ERC 721 NFTs will also impact demand by incorporating historical ownership creating a subclass of crypto-assets called cryptocollectables.
>
> In addition, a currently underutilised token model is the crypto-consumable, a token that is programmed to reduce in value over time using a decay or burn function. This could be a continuous decline in value like a used car or a steep decline like a ticket to a live event. This sort of token design would not be a store-of-value and would be a powerful way to increase network token velocity.
>
> ...
>
> Tokens are the first native coordination mechanism for the digital and now machine economy. We expect tokens to be issued at each layer of the stack to incentivise behaviours within each particular network and to connect with the broader ecosystem through a series of exchanges and interoperability protocols. The model would be similar to today's global economy in which each nation issues and uses their own currency within their own borders and trades foreign currency with other countries for products and services that it needs. If Bitcoin is indeed the digital store-of-value in the same way gold is the physical store-of-value, it is likely we will see a digital hierarchy of money emerge with Bitcoin as an apex token, protocol tokens like Ethereum, NEO and Cardano below Bitcoin, and utility or application tokens

below the protocol tokens. As the Convergence economy develops and core infrastructure is developed, tokens will become increasingly liquid and frictionless leading to extraordinarily complex economic dynamics.

Nick Tomaino, founder @1confirmation, proposes a model with a somewhat different classification where tokens offer four types of fundamental value:

The four major token types are: traditional asset tokens, usage tokens, work tokens, and hybrid tokens.

Token type	Function	Examples
Traditional asset token	To represent a traditional asset cryptographically	USDT, DGD
Usage token	To provide access to a digital service	BTC, ETH, BAT
Work token	To provide the right to contribute work to a decentralized organization	REP, MKR
Hybrid (usage + work)	To provide access to a digital service and the right to contribute work	FIL, ETH (with Casper)

The token type that has obvious fundamental value is any type of traditional asset token that cryptographically represents underlying traditional assets such as equity, real estate, gold, etc. The value underlying tokenised traditional assets is well understood ... I think we will see a proliferation of traditional asset tokens as regulatory clarity increases because of the liquidity and global nature of tokens on blockchains.

...

A usage token is a token where a digital service is offered and the token is required to access that digital service that no centralised party controls ... The fundamental value of usage tokens is determined by the uniqueness of the resources underlying the digital service and the utility of the decentralised digital service itself ... Bitcoin is the best-known example of a usage token to date

...

A work token is a token that gives token holders the right to contribute work to a decentralised organisation to help enable that decentralised organisation to function. In some cases there are fees rewarded for that work, but not always. The fundamental value of a work token is determined by the utility that token holders get from the decentralised organisation. That utility can come in the form of fees (a more direct utility) or goodwill (a less direct utility). Work tokens are far less understood than traditional asset tokens and usage tokens to date. There are a few good examples of work tokens, like Augur's Reputation (REP), and Maker DAO's Maker (MKR), but not many.

...

Many future (hybrid) tokens may function as both usage and work tokens. When Ethereum switches from proof-of-work to proof-of-stake, ETH will be both a usage token (you need gas to use the EVM) and a work token (ETH gives you the right to validate transactions and earn in exchange for that work).

These insights represent some typical views into the nature of tokens and are crucial to thinking about their valuations. Extensive literature is being published daily, but what is no longer in doubt is that tokens add significant value to a network which did not exist prior to them. They can be designed for different utilities and are digital assets in themselves, and their value can change over time as network effects kick-in or falter.

But determining a "market value" for different tokens, let alone a theoretical price, as with stock futures and options, is challenging and easier said than done, not the least due to the "mania" enveloping ICOs and the sheer gush of money flowing in.

Simple, common-sense yardsticks which should be evident to all and sundry are not being employed with token valuations resulting in a definite mis-pricing.

Mis-pricing in ICOs

One reason for mis-pricing and the principal problem with ICOs is that the amount of money being raised is simply decoupled from the actual cash needs of the blockchain startups. Too much money is just as bad as too little money, and over-funded companies lack financial discipline or hire too many people too fast and lose focus on the product. Most ICOs are based on little more than a white paper, and it's quite unlikely that at the end of the day investors will have much to celebrate.

Then there is the law of all startups to contend with — blockchain or otherwise — that 90% of them will fail (it could have been 89 or 91, but apparently the decentralised, immutable consensus in startup literature stands at 90%). Hence, even with proper due diligence, successful ICOs will lead to successful outcomes only in one of ten blockchain startups.

Another reason, as our case studies in Maslow's Hammer clearly illustrate, is that many ideas don't need a blockchain solution or an ICO at all. They are suited to centralised database implementation, have no particular need for a community, and sometimes have no real business model either. You cannot decentralise everything for the sake of it. Such tokens are bound to be rendered meaningless in due course.

The teams behind the ICOs usually have nothing to lose; once the millions or billions have been raised, there is no significant pressure to execute and deliver on their idea. There is no governance on the use of funds. Compare this to typical startups where entrepreneurs get a modest valuation and have to be "all-in" the project to see any returns after five to ten years of hard work. They are forever on-the-hook.

The lack of regulation, accountability and legal structures makes it the "wild-west" of finance; a topic explored in detail later in this chapter. It dramatically impacts the probability of success. The sizeable amount of money sloshing around is like a magnet to fraudsters, even as regulators like the SEC are now stepping in to fill the vacuum. To corroborate this statistically, figures put out by the China Academy of Information and Communications Technology (CAICT) say that of the 80,000 blockchain projects ever launched globally, only 8% are still being actively maintained today, and the average lifespan is only around 1.22 years. Similarly, data from the ICO tracking site TokenData shows that of the startups that launched ICOs last year, 142 of them failed at the funding stage while another 276 eventually faded into obscurity or simply took the money and ran. In a study released in January 2018, Ernst & Young said more than 10 per cent of funds raised through ICOs were either lost or stolen in hacker attacks.

Besides these, there are other questions that need to be figured out in any token sale whose answers will be far from obvious:

> Is the design and structure of the token sale the best possible of all options? For example, could it be better to port the smart contracts of a token to use ether directly, instead of creating a new token per protocol?
> Is the token akin to an investment security, that is, is it an ICO masquerading as an IPO?
> Do the investors have any legal safeguards in the ICO?
> Are the investors entitled to any dividend-like payouts?
> Can the token holders exercise control in the protocol or application via voting rights?

An interesting comparison would be to look at the relatively mature startup funding process which has evolved into set global practices over decades. Startups typically raise initial funding from founders in the friends-and-family round in the range of US$5,000 to US$100,000 at the idea stage. Angel funding from High-Net-Worth Individuals (HNIs) comes in once the startup grows and delivers some product prototype, some client revenue or some other traction like the number of application downloads or user sign-ups. It usually happens in the second or third year, and the amount being raised may vary between US$25,000 to US$500,000. Then follows the Series A Venture Capital funding, somewhere between 2-5 years of the business having been in existence and having strong traction in all aspects like its team, products and revenue per user. The amount raised may vary between US$1m to US$10m. Series B and other subsequent rounds of funding come typically after 1-2 years of the last round and are again based on the traction gained and need for funds. It is worth noting that more than eighty percent startups who raise one round of funding do not get to the next round on account of failures in between.

Contrast this model with Blockchain startups which have launched ICOs and raised capital in millions and billions of dollars at the idea stage itself. For example, the Cayman Islands startup Block.one raised US$4 billion till May 2018 in its year-long ICO for its blockchain platform eos.ios without even a live flagship product. Money poured in only on the promise that its founders, who have run other well-known blockchain projects, would repeat their success. Similarly, the group behind the messaging app Telegram raised US$1.7 billion in token sales from private investors but shelved its plans for an ICO. All this, when over fifty per cent of the ICOs from 2017 had already failed — ONECOIN which had raised US$350 million without a business or white paper and proved to be a scam, Coindash and Veritaseum which lost US$10 million and US$8 million to hackers respectively, and many others.

Ironically, having completed its massive ICO on Ethereum's ERC20 network, Block.one later announced its migration to its network ESOIO, dumping Ethereum and moving all its users and coins. It emerged as a significant threat to Ethereum and the value of ether as it implied that eos.ios would sell its massive holding of 916,000 ETH in the wallet address EOS-Owner, with an additional 237,000 ETH which it had realised from the

ICO over the year. Such is the price to be paid for openness and decentralisation. To view it in perspective, in a centralised world where Facebook and Apple charge over 30% of the revenue from companies for the use of their platforms, an event of this nature would not have been possible.

On a side note, the crypto craze sweeping the world culminated in several weird and wonderful advertising campaigns, featuring some exciting celebrities and big businesses, including world-renowned footballer Lio Messi endorsing a company producing blockchain hardware, while flamboyant boxer Floyd Mayweather entered the fray with an Ethereum-based ICO, along with Paris Hilton and footballer Luis Suraez. Stevan Seagal promoted an ICO that was halted after a regulatory order. Besides celebrities, several entrepreneurs and corporate honchos like John McAfee became "ICO Advisors" and lent their profiles for ICO projects, in return for ICO tokens and other fiat/crypto currencies to help beef-up the image of an ICO project.

Of course, the question of regulation remains the proverbial elephant in the blockchain room — a question we now examine.

Regulation of ICOs

Ever since the Solomon vs Solomon ruling in 1896 which segregated the personal liability of a shareholder from the company's liability, the ICO is probably the most innovative corporate-structure concept that will stand out in hindsight and will be used in the future.

As of today, the legal state of ICOs is mostly undefined. Crypto tokens are not securities in the traditional sense unless they are specifically employed in a way to raise funds substituting for an IPO. Ideally, the token sells not as a financial asset but as a digital good. Forcing tokens to comply within the existing securities framework can destroy their potential. As would be expected, regulators and governments in different countries have reacted differently to the ICO boom and to bitcoins and altcoins in general — some welcoming, some unsure and some who have imposed outright bans and clampdowns.

In the US, the Securities and Exchange Commission (SEC) has stepped in majorly to end the wild-west phase of crypto. Way back in July 2017, the SEC had ruled that tokens offered and sold by a "virtual" organisation known as "The DAO" were securities and therefore subject to the federal securities laws. Their report confirmed that issuers of distributed ledger or blockchain technology-based securities must register offers and the sales of such securities unless a valid exemption applied. Those taking part in unregistered offerings may also be held liable for violations of the securities laws. Additionally, securities exchanges providing for trading in these securities must register unless they are exempt.

It is unlikely that the SEC can chase every fraudulent token sale and dealing with owner anonymity compounds the problem – since coin owners are typically a unique private address on the internet. Hence it makes sense to regulate where these tokens live — the coin exchanges — who are now under pressure to perform full KYC of their users.

Another instance where the SEC came down heavily was when it was alleged that the tokens sold to US investors during Tezos' ICO were actually securities. Tezos had raised a record-breaking $232 million during its ICO in July 2017 and became a subject of scrutiny and multiple lawsuits over the question of its compliance with the SEC regulations. Since the company had not registered themselves with the SEC it amounted to a securities fraud.

A vital court precedent — the Howey test — is being used as a benchmark to establish whether an ICO will be considered a security from the SEC perspective. Essentially there are four criteria that need to be met for a token to be declared a security:

> There is an investment of money.
> There is an expectation of profits.
> The investment of money is in a common enterprise.
> Any profit comes from the efforts of a promoter or a third party.

Hence tokens like bitcoin, litecoin, bitcoin cash and dash easily clear the Howey test and are not securities. So also is the case with Ethereum and its token ether. But many other coins like NEO, one of 2017's biggest ICOs and frequently dubbed "Chinese Ethereum," precisely hit the SEC's definition of a security since the NEO coin gives an owner shares in the company.

Nick Tomaino suggests the possibility that many more founders could go the Satoshi route of being completely anonymous upon launch to allow their tokens to maintain broad accessibility and also to avoid any regulatory risk. He feels that if regulators come down aggressively and declare all tokens as securities, there is a strong chance that this will come to pass.

The US Congress is also taking an active interest in the subject, for example, on March 14, 2018, its Subcommittee on Capital Markets, Securities and Investment held a hearing titled "Examining the Crypto currencies and ICO Markets," the first of many such hearings. At the moment they have yielded more questions than answers on the subject of regulation.

Canada, meanwhile, issued regulations saying that each token is unique and should be evaluated on its characteristics. It then went on to list the exact same conditions as the Howey test. (CSA staff notice, 46–307 "Crypto currency offerings" as released by CSA Canada).

Both Facebook and Google in early-2018 announced a ban on all types of advertisements for crypto currencies and ICOs. The Reserve Bank of India ordered all Indian banks to disallow people from using their credit cards and bank accounts to invest in crypto currencies and ICOs. China and South Korea had already banned ICOs in 2017 itself. All these measures did not have much impact on the prices of crypto currencies though.

On the other hand, within a month of the Chinese, Japan's Financial Services Agency officially endorsed eleven companies as operators of crypto currency exchanges and did not ban ICOs at all. It is possible that the Chinese and Korean measures were just precursors till regulations and policies for ICOs could be put in place by both governments.

Meanwhile, Gibraltar and Estonia, like Japan, are among the few countries that have allowed ICO fundraising. In Spain, the People's Party is preparing legislation including possible tax breaks for companies that will use blockchain technology, while Switzerland introduced new guidelines on ICOs, each falling within one or more categories: payment, asset, utility. And last but not the least, Malta has introduced regulations heavily in favour of crypto currency companies.

Regulation implies "mainstreaming" and "integration" of crypto currencies with the traditional financial markets. For example, Morgan Stanley has announced trading in complex derivatives tied to the largest crypto currencies, giving their investors synthetic exposure contracts to the performance of bitcoin. The bank is also prepared to offer bitcoin swap trading tied to bitcoin future contracts for a spread charge.

Goldman Sachs and Citigroup are also preparing new products tied to bitcoin (Report in the *Economic Times* dated Sep 14, 2018).

Apart from the legal and regulatory aspects of the ICOs, there are philosophical questions relating to the law in the context of the blockchain itself. Blockchains based systems act autonomously bypassing the existing state-based jurisdictions and regulatory mechanisms in place. People are free to construct their systems of rules enforced by the underlying protocol of the blockchain network. As elegantly stated by Primavera De Felippi and Aaron Wright in *Blockchain and the Law*:

> These systems create order without law and implement what can be thought of as private regulatory frameworks.

And again:

> We could increasingly subject ourselves to the "rule of code" — code that may not be controlled by any one party and that may or may not operate in accordance with the "rule of law".

Security Token Offerings (STOs) a.k.a. Reverse ICOs

A late development and a hybrid product of pure crypto tokens and traditional securities (or shares) is the Security Token Offering, also being called as reverse ICOs. Whereas tokens or coins in a conventional ICO are offered in exchange for other crypto currencies, typically bitcoins and ether, there aren't any associated rights and obligations, and the newly acquired tokens can only be used to access the specific platform, service or network. Traditional financial securities like shares and bonds are always backed by tangible assets of the company issuing them and meet all compliance and regulatory standards.

STOs attempt to bridge the two and offer the best of both worlds to the investors. In reality, it is just a natural fall-out of the tightening noose of regulators around ICOs as discussed above, and may be a way to re-brand the inevitable fact that most ICOs in the future will be treated as an issue of securities from the regulatory viewpoint and issuers will be held liable against applicable laws.

STOs are also being promoted as a solution for existing old-world companies with strong revenue streams to raise funds through coin offerings while remaining fully compliant with their existing obligations under securities laws. The tokens can be listed on separate SEC certified exchanges to create an alternative to the traditional stock market.

As with any hybrid, there will always be a trade-off in the design of such tokens. The more they try to mimic traditional securities, the more centralised they will be, and the more sheen they lose of being on the blockchain. In any case, here it will be regulators calling the shots rather than the other way round.

Crypto Exchange-Traded Funds (ETFs)

ETFs are great enablers — investors can participate by proxy in a wide range of worldwide markets trading in commodities, stocks and derivatives. It would have been inevitable that the first Crypto ETF would come into being touting the benefits and ease of investing in a basket of crypto currencies. Certain advantages are obvious. Security for one, since digital wallets and crypto exchanges are always prone to breaches, while an investor in the crypto ETF has an added layer of security in the custodian bank that supports the ETF.

An example of a fund that acts like an ETF is the Bitcoin Investment Trust (GBTC) which owns bitcoins on the behalf of its investors and allows them to trade in shares of the trust. However, it is listed outside the US, since so far the US SEC has not approved such ETFs in principle.

In Aug 2108, the SEC gave a much-awaited ruling on pending Bitcoin ETF proposals rejecting them on common grounds. The ruling made it clear that the rejection was not on the ground as to whether bitcoin had value as an investment, but on the point that none of the crypto exchanges had demonstrated their ability to prevent fraudulent practices, and that the bitcoin futures markets were not significant in size. Included in the rejected proposals was one by the Winklevoss twins for the second time. Nevertheless, crypto enthusiasts hope to cross this hurdle in due course.

Be that as it may, there is an interesting parallel here with the Global Financial Crisis of 2008 and its now infamous Collateralized Debt Obligations (CDOs), which were structured financial products that pooled together various cashflow-generating assets and repackaged the pool into discrete tranches that were sold to investors. As CDOs grew and flourished, their structure became ever more elaborate, with the newer CDOs-squared comprising of the middle tranches of other multiple CDOs, all aggregated to create more "risk-free" investments for banks, hedge funds and other large investors. The middle tranches of even these were not spared and then further combined into a still more abstract instrument called CDO-cubed. By this point, the returns were three times removed from the underlying home mortgages. What followed when millions of home mortgages defaulted, was the most spectacular bust in the so-called "risk-free" CDOs.

The risk in the structuring of Crypto ETFs is even more striking. At least the bottom-layer in the CDOs comprised real mortgage securities. The tokens that would form the pool of most Crypto ETFs are themselves virtual assets whose valuation is hard to ascertain. We have already discussed in detail the prevalent mis-pricing, the lack of regulation and mass euphoria driving crypto prices. Adding another layer of abstraction to what is already abstract at its core, and then pricing it, is a foolhardy exercise to say the least, especially in light of our past experiences with CDOs. But the gush of money on the sidelines poised to enter various crypto ETFs seems to suggest that we are doomed to repeat our mistakes.

Crypto Insurance and Crypto Custody

Where there is a risk, there will be insurance. Crypto risks have engendered a hot new business that more and more firms are looking to get into — crypto insurance. While the lack of regulation in this domain is the biggest pitfall, and the high ratio of frauds and scams the next big trap, the sheer size and prospects of crypto currencies are too attractive for insurers who are betting they can avoid these pitfalls. The premiums from insuring such risks can be substantial, and by some accounts, underwriters charge a blockchain company upwards of five times or more than the average risk premium for coverage against loss or theft.

Marsh & McLennan and Aon are amongst the two leading insurance brokers that help companies shop for crypto policies, and claim to be doing good business. Aon claims to have over 50 percent of the market for crypto insurance.

American International Group (AIG) has also been adding crypto coverage into its standard policy forms. So far, there do not appear to be any claims that any insurer has had to pay on account of crypto policies despite the headlines about crypto hacks and thefts.

Another nascent field that is just evolving is regulated crypto custody. As numerous crypto currency custody services are now under development and testing, including one at Coinbase Inc., they bode well for the crypto market's future since custodianship is a crucial problem that needs a solution if large amounts of capital are to flow into crypto currencies.

While investment bank Nomura Holdings Inc. has joined hands to create a custody consortium called Komainu, at least three other giant Wall Street custodians — Bank of New York Mellon Corp., JPMorgan Chase & Co. and Northern Trust Corp. — are working on crypto custody services or exploring it.

This mechanism would also allow hedge funds and pension funds to invest in bitcoins and altcoins, as well as enable retail brokerages to let clients add crypto to their stock portfolios. About US$20 billion in crypto assets are poised to flow into custody services once they're available, estimates Coinbase.

As someone put it succinctly — if you want to start a crypto business that everyone will need in the future, solve the inheritance problem. Everyone will pay you gladly.

The study of legal and regulatory aspects of the blockchain is just in its infancy, as are the theoretical foundations for pricing ICOs, digital tokens, crypto insurance and crypto custody. There are many other technologies further queering the field, such as Artificial Intelligence and the Internet of Things, the intersection of which with the blockchain forms the subject of our last chapter. It is, however, the pace of the transformation that threatens to create a regulatory void, a period of volatility and surprises as technology continues to outpace regulation by a mile.

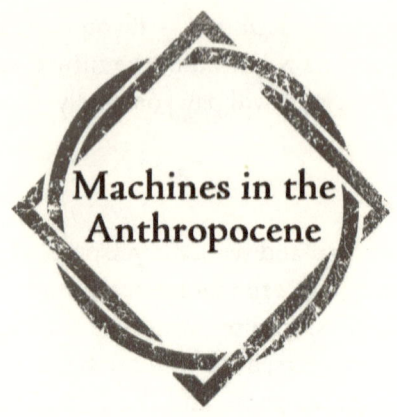

Machines in the Anthropocene

Blockchain as Futuristic Technology

> We drive into the future using only our rear-view mirror.
> — Marshall McLuhan

Christopher Nolan's 2014 dystopian sci-fi film *Interstellar* is the story of a group of astronauts who travel through space in search of a planet where humanity can be translocated since the Earth is being rendered uninhabitable. Kip Thorne, a theoretical physicist, was the film's scientific consultant and executive producer, and laid down that nothing in the film would violate physical laws while speculations would spring from science and not wild imagination. This film set the bar for what the future of space travel could be like. Theoretical physicist Michio Kaku praised the film highly for its scientific accuracy, and said that *Interstellar* "could set the gold standard for science fiction movies for years to come" (Wikipedia).

In the film, faced with unknown situations and dangers as they explore potential planets, the crew of four and their two robots — TARS and CASE — confront some tough decisions to be made which materially affects the success of their mission. Even as they scientifically analyse each situation and work out probabilities based on the data assimilated by their robots, the scenes highlight gripping emotions always at play underlying their decisions.

In reality, unmanned missions will lead space exploration in the future, where more than humans, it will be machines that will face unknown scenarios and will have to come up with some split-second decisions based on data they gather and probabilities they compute. These machines have to communicate, cooperate and act on data in coordination with each other. So how will this real-time data from a scenario be shared, analysed and acted upon in consensus between different algorithms driving diverse machines from multiple manufacturers or even countries, located apart in space and time?

Believe it or not, but a future version of the blockchain would be our best bet into making this scenario feasible. Shared immutable data, consensus between dissimilar nodes without the need for trust, distributed programs whose code cannot be altered — sounds familiar or wishful?

From "Houston, We Have a Solution: Blockchain in the Space Industry" by Stephen O'Neal (Aug 6, 2018, *Cointelegraph*):

> In 2017, NASA awarded a $330,000 grant that supported the development of an autonomous, blockchain-based spacecraft system, making its first move toward blockchain adoption. Called the Resilient Networking and Computing Paradigm (RNCP), the new system relies on blockchain and requires no human intervention, as the grant's recipient, Dr Jin Wei Kocsis — an assistant professor of electrical and computer engineering at the University of Akron — outlines in her research synopsis.
>
> As Kocsis explains, the RNCP will examine the application of Ethereum-based blockchain smart contracts in developing a secure computing system that would be applicable for challenging space conditions:
>
>> "In this project, the Ethereum blockchain technology will be exploited to develop a decentralised,

secure, and cognitive networking and computing infrastructure for deep space exploration. The blockchain consensus protocols will be further explored to improve the resilience of the infrastructure[...] I hope to develop technology that can recognise environmental threats and avoid them, as well as complete a number of tasks automatically."

In more detail, the RNCP system will exploit smart contracts to build a spacecraft that would automatically and promptly detect and dodge any hindrance — as in deep space, conventional means of communication become less reliable as the signal gets weaker. Thus, Dr Kocsis hopes that, equipped with this blockchain solution, spacecraft will be able to complete more tasks, provide more data and give scientists more time for information analysis, as they would not have to spend time on detecting potential environmental threats. No specific timeline has been disclosed thus far.

The blog-post also talks about ideas such as a distant blockchain that is powered by satellites and a decentralised autonomous organisation (DAO) that will allow settlers to 3-D print infrastructure on the lunar surface.

So once we conquer the Moon, as NASA believes, will Mars be far behind? Future space colonies will be modelled here and now, and the blockchain technology shall help humans to re-imagine the society of the future. But before we conquer space, let us talk about our terrestrial web.

Web 3.0

Web 3.0 is unfolding before our eyes now; we are a part of it as are technologies like the blockchain. It's just that from the middle it is very easy to miss the wood for the trees. The infrastructure being built using blockchains as a core will take a few years to mature and stabilise for mission-critical distributed applications. By then the hype would have largely dissipated. A "token crash" that may be in the offing would be part of the maturing. But the tokens that survive this crash will be the tokens of tomorrow, just as a Google or Amazon survived the dotcom crash to become the giants of Web 2.0.

Are there features of this transition we can see today? Absolutely.

For one, blockchain will be one of the foundational technologies of the future, a backbone like the internet itself. The intersection of Artificial Intelligence (AI), Blockchain technology, Internet of Things (IoT) and advances in Quantum Computing is an extremely potent mix. While impossible to predict in terms of how it will play out, play out it will. The digital economy will give way to the machine economy — commerce through tokens will be a native part of machine-to-machine and human-to-machine interactions. From *The Convergence Ecosystem* — "The Ecosystem sees data captured by the Internet of Things, managed by block-chains, automated by artificial intelligence, and all incentivised using crypto-tokens. The Convergence Ecosystem is open source, distributed, decentralised, automated and tokenised and we believe it is nothing less than an economic paradigm shift."

Two, users will be in control of their data. It will be the single most definitive feature of Web 3.0. Whether users are willing to part with their data for services or targeted advertising or crypto-money will be a matter of individual choice, and not dictated by the compulsions of using a particular network. The internet platforms of the future will be more open.

Three, society will be very different. That's a truism as well. But crypto feeds directly into the gig economy. As AI picks up the slack, the man-machine partnership will be the way forward.

Four, crypto currencies will be mainstream and ubiquitous, and governments all over the world will launch fiat crypto currencies or fiat digital currencies, whether out of compulsion or choice. Since governments have the power of taxation, and they can declare any digital token as legal tender for payment of taxes, they can have fiat tokens. But it will take time before central banks can make this transition, not only because the economic effects of crypto are sizeable and mostly unknowable, capable of impacting the stability of nation-states, but also because they are "central" by definition and cannot appreciate anything as decentralised as crypto currencies. But one way or the other, along with Bitcoins, we will definitely have the BitDollars, BitPounds, BitEuros, BitYens and BitYuans of the world.

A live laboratory for the crypto currency experiment today is Venezuela, where hyperinflation has ruined the value of its fiat currency (Bolivar), and the government has launched its crypto currency — the Petro — to compete with bitcoin which is the currency of choice of the people.

Machines calling Machines

Automation will cause a dramatic shift away from the advertising-driven business model of Web 2.0.

Imagine being seated in the back of a Tesla self-driving car and initiating a voice search (as in Siri or Alexa) for your destination. The Tesla voice assistant searches Google for information on that place, but in return for Google's search service, Tesla does not see any advertisements since machines are impervious to them, unlike humans. Hence, internet advertising cannot be a compensation and Google may be paid in some crypto currency like bitcoins, or possibly Google's own G-coins in return for the micro-service rendered.

And unlike today, Google may also credit Tesla with some G-coins or T-coins (Tesla coins) for selecting the relevant search result because that is how Google's algorithms benefit from knowing the right answer through crowdsourcing, making for more relevant search results. The internet's free business model based on advertising will not hold as machines start interacting with machines.

The world's digital currencies may not just be BitDollars or BitPounds, but could well be T-coins for Tesla, A-coins for Amazon, and G-coins for Google. What's more, these digital currencies would be continuously and automatically exchanged between machines on behalf of humans as micro-services and products change hands.

Digital Assets, Cryptokitties and Gaming

We can also catch glimpses of the development of "personal digital assets" where blockchain will indeed play a unique role, such as the use of non-fungible blockchain tokens (NFTs) to create and track these unique digital assets. Most tokens, like the bitcoin (BTC) are fungible tokens, that is, all BTC tokens are the same and interchangeable. But by using the scripting language of the Bitcoin blockchain to add a layer on top of the native protocol, it can also serve as a ledger that maintains ownership of NFTs. And just as the ERC20 token standard on Ethereum kick-started the boom in tokens and ICOs, its ERC-721 standard, and the more recent ERC1155, is doing the same for NFTs.

Cryptokitties — unique virtual cats that can be created on the Ethereum network — is arguably the most famous use-case of NFTs for digital collectables so far. It may appear as a fad, but it establishes the technology for the creation of scarce digital assets that anyone in the world can own on a decentralised trustless network. Not only can you customise the appearance and growth of the cats, but you can also mate them with each other to produce kittens having features inherited from their parents. All these developments portend well for the future in the case of intellectual property and copyright management.

Gamers have been amongst the earliest adopters of crypto currency since most games are based on a token-reward system, anyway. Besides, blockchains can provide gamers with a host of non-fungible assets including game skins and virtual cards which have verifiable scarcity based on NFTs. Exchanging such in-game assets is a lucrative industry estimated at some US$50 billion currently and growing rapidly in the future, and facilitating this are platforms like Wax, OpenSea and Rare Bits. These decentralised asset exchanges can become tomorrow's bustling marketplaces in various industries from financial assets to physical assets tied to a blockchain.

ICOs - The Future of Corporate Structures

Currently, a company has different stakeholders like shareholders, employees, vendors and consumers, and their interests are usually not aligned with each other; sometimes they are in outright conflict. ICOs may help evolve a solution by merging all stake-holders into a single community driven by a common token. It needs willingness amongst community members to decentralise control, away from large corporations, and have all stakeholders work towards a common goal with an economic incentive.

In the past, open source movements like Wikipedia, Linux and other crowdsourcing projects have worked successfully even without a financial incentive. But many other open source projects failed due to lack of such goodwill and commitment on the part of the community. ICO tokens can add the missing economic incentives in such cases and help blur the boundaries between different types of stakeholders, leading to a vibrant token economy.

Depending on how ICO regulation finds its feet, ICOs can offer fair and equal access to investors around the world. From a venture capitalist in Silicon Valley to a fund manager in

London, to a small retail investor in Vietnam, all could have an equal opportunity to invest in such crypto assets.

Intermediaries Disintermediated

Uber could be decentralised by a community and token-driven foundation that matches riders and drivers with a standard set of fair, transparent and community agreed parameters, such as how much to charge per passenger per distance, how much to pay each driver, etcetera. It would differ from Uber-like companies because it would not burn any cash in the process of creating a market, nor squeeze drivers and consumers to return shareholder profits. It is likely to work sustainably as long as its community's governance is well-managed.

A similar fate could await all other intermediaries of Web 2.0 including Airbnb, Lyft, OneFineStay, Etsy and many others.

Self-sovereign Identity

Self-sovereign identity will be a core feature of Web 3.0 through which individuals can authenticate and verify themselves without having to pass on their documents. Blockchains would make it possible for individuals and institutions to attest each other through a peer-to-peer mechanism, and store their data securely, with encryption, in decentralised apps, shredded across the cloud, at a reasonable cost.

Firms like Cove Identity (*full disclosure — I'm a co-founder here*) and several others are like Evernym, their not-for-profit twin Sovrin, Civic, SelfKey, etcetera are at advanced stages of making this work.

Once self-sovereign identity becomes the norm, individuals will have the ability to track instances where a third-party sells their personal information, and services will enable payment for sharing their details without losing control of the data. Automated systems such as chatbots, companions and AI advisors can increase authentication and, in some cases, verification.

The blockchain token is at the heart of the blockchain ledger and, at the cost of repeating ourselves, the newest beast on the block.

We have analysed its origin and transformation, rise and fall, and its strengths and weaknesses from many angles, including as a currency, as a facilitator for dApps and smart contracts, as an incentive for triggering the network effect while creating new open networks, and in fund-raising through ICOs.

A lot of these roles can and do overlap in different blockchain projects and applications, giving rise to many innovative ideas, and some old wine in new bottles.

Much like the Internet in 1998, the blockchain's potential is much more significant and different than we imagine, and not entirely relevant in many of our current use-cases in today's centralised offline/online world. Its adoption is likely to be driven by future technologies, even as it plays a role in the future of technology.

Our whole effort in Squaring the Blockchain Circle has been about gaining the right insights that can stimulate new thinking, because like the blind men of Indostan in our introduction, our beast too defies encapsulation.

When human beings discovered the first stone-age tools, human society experienced the most fundamental of changes — from cave dwellers to organised communities. The Palaeolithic age lasted well over two million years before the dawn of agriculture marked the Neolithic Age and another dramatic shift in human history.

Flash forward to the age of the Anthropocene where we humans have so profoundly impacted the Earth that it has altered nature's trajectory, all within the last hundred odd years. Technology has played an incredible role in this jump, and this accelerating timeline has been punctuated by many a fundamental breakthrough, both big and small.

The blockchain ranks there with the best. Posterity shall gratefully remember Satoshi Nakamoto, and his legacy and followers.

I hope you enjoyed reading this book.

About the Author

Kunal is a startup entrepreneur, the founder and CEO of two Fintech firms, uTrade Solutions — an algorithmic trading firm, and Hashcove — a UK-based blockchain solutions firm.

Kunal is also a co-founder of the Chandigarh Angels Network in India, and of Earthr.org, an upcoming sustainability-focussed crowdsourcing social platform.

Previously Kunal has worked in Investment Banking and Capital Markets in Lehman Brothers, Nomura and BNP Paribas in London.

He holds a Computer Science Engineering degree from PEC, Chandigarh, India, and an MBA from ESSEC, Paris, France.

Kunal is now working on his second book which is due to be published in the first-half of 2019. It is focused on helping startups succeed against the odds while solving "real-world" problems that tackle issues related to the environment and sustainability. From the blurb of the forthcoming book:

> Startups form a separate industry in their own right, and every individual, whether a graduate, drop-out, technocrat or professional has a choice to be an entrepreneur.
> Statistically, more than 90% of startups shut within the first three years. But a new bunch of startups launch every day, drawing inspiration from a handful of successful ones that ran the gauntlet and made it big.
> Since the odds are so low, would it not be appropriate to seek the strength to succeed from our a higher motivation behind the startup, beyond money, such as a passion for solving a problem or learning anew? If we are likely to fail why fail at something small? Why implement another little me-too, low value-added business idea? Why not try to solve the real, significant problems we humans face that go beyond the usual themes of e-commerce, on-demand services, internet

apps, etcetera?

The book is in two sections. The first section highlights several such sustainability challenges and their corresponding potential startup ideas that can be scaled into businesses while solving real problems. It's harder to solve these problems compared to build-run-exit internet startups, but they are worth trying, even at the cost of failure. Classic successful examples of such businesses include Aravind Eyecare, Tesla Motors, Khan Academy and BeyondMeat.

The second section drills down on what is necessary to run such startups. How to maximise the probability of falling into the 10% band of successful startups? It unfolds the knacks and hacks for team-building, fund-raising, selling and scaling-up.

In a line, this book aims to inspire you with a higher motivation for your startup while giving you the edge needed to succeed.

www.ingramcontent.com/pod-product-compliance
Lightning Source LLC
Chambersburg PA
CBHW031414210526
45464CB00005B/1878